The Prepper's
Cookbook

**300 Recipes to Turn
Your Emergency Food
into Nutritious, Delicious,
Life-Saving Meals**

Tess Pennington

Ulysses Press

Published by:
Ulysses Press
P.O. Box 3440
Berkeley, CA 94703
www.ulyssespress.com

A Hollan Publishing, Inc. Concept

ISBN: 978-1-61243-129-1
Library of Congress Catalog Number 2012951892

Printed in Canada by Marquis Book Printing

10 9 8 7 6 5 4 3 2

Acquisitions Editor: Keith Riegert
Managing Editor: Claire Chun
Editor: Phyllis Elving
Proofreader: Elyce Berrigan-Dunlop
Cover design: what!design @ whatweb.com
Interior design and production: Jake Flaherty
Cover photos: chili con carne © Ingrid Balabanova/shutterstock.com; jarred peppers © Lincoln Rogers/shutterstock.com; peach cobbler © Charles Brutlag/shutterstock.com
Interior illustrations: page 5: camping equipment © Rusty Letter Images; page 12: propane cooker © Zern Liew/shutterstock.com; page 42: glass jars © Rusty Letter Images; page 87: waffles © Rusty Letter Images; page 98: pot © AKaiser/shutterstock.com; page 115: groceries © Retro Clip Art/shutterstock.com; page 137: saucepan © Rusty Letter Images; page 146: boy © Rusty Letter Images; page 154: vegetables © bioraven/shutterstock.com; page 167: wheat © Rusty Letter Images; page 175: bread © Canicula/shutterstock.com; page 187: pie © bioraven/shutterstock.com; page 204: kettle © AKaiser/shutterstock.com; page 209: cans © Oleg Iatsun/shutterstock.com

Distributed by Publishers Group West

NOTE TO READERS: This book is independently authored and published and no sponsorship or endorsement of this book by, and no affiliation with, any trademarked brand of alcoholic beverages or other products mentioned or pictured within is claimed or suggested. All trademarks that appear in ingredient lists, photographs, and elsewhere in this book belong to their respective owners and are used here for informational purposes only. The authors and publishers encourage readers to patronize the quality brands of alcoholic beverages and other products mentioned and pictured in this book.

TABLE OF CONTENTS

1 INTRODUCTION TO PREPPING

Throughout my childhood, I heard stories of how my pioneering great-great-grandmother, Lillie May Busby, drove a covered wagon across Oklahoma to Texas with her seventeen children. In these stories, she often set up camp and fed her family. The members of my family knew how to make do with very little, but they were somehow able to generate enough food to feed a hungry family. As my grandmother once said, "We were very poor, but our love for each other made us rich."

I come from a generous, loving family, and they have passed down their recipes as gifts to be shared with the younger generations. My family is my inspiration for this book, and it is my firm belief that they would enjoy sharing their gifts with you.

WE ARE NEO-PIONEERS!

Homesteading, self-reliance, and what many of us call "prepping" is really neo-pioneerism. When early Americans migrated westward, they had to adapt to a new environment, and their supplies had to become multifunctional. Their wherewithal to live on very little by using the available resources is something to marvel at. Pioneers lived on the food they produced, and a portion of their harvest was put aside for future use.

Don't wait for an emergency to venture back to our pioneering past and to live simply. Start practicing these skills now in order to have them in place—along with the necessary supplies—when a disaster or unexpected emergency does strike.

As a child, I'd watch my grandmother stockpile plastic containers that food came in. This seemed odd to me, but I attributed her behavior to having grown up during the Great Depression. I see it differently today. There's always another use or a second purpose for an item.

The ability to adapt to situations was another concept that kept our ancestors flourishing. This adaptability carried through to the foods they stored. Their cellars and storage rooms were stocked with versatile yet compatible foods, and they made the most of limited space.

EVERY FAMILY SHOULD PREPARE

With the increase of natural and man-made disasters, many people feel that it's time to get preparations together. Being prepared for emergencies that may directly affect you and your family is like purchasing an insurance policy. When you need those preparations the most, they'll be there for you. How comforting is that?

This book will help you make the most of your preparedness supplies by giving you tips on how to preserve food just as your ancestors did. You'll find a list of foods to have in an emergency food pantry, and I share many favorite recipes for using them. It's my intention to help each and every one of you to thrive during an emergency—with supplies and tools in place—so that it will be more of a minor inconvenience than a major setback.

We've witnessed first-hand how unprepared our society is to handle disasters, natural or man-made. Sadly, for the majority of us, we will watch as the disasters play out time and again on our televisions. Yet we fail to realize that this is not some distant phenomenon that can't happen in our neighborhoods and communities. We haven't yet learned the importance of being prepared.

It is a societal taboo to think in terms of worst-case scenarios. When we do, we're likely to be labeled "paranoid." But accepting that disasters happen should define us as being prudent, not paranoid. Good planning leads to a good response, and the more planning you've done, the more steadfast you'll be in your response to a disaster.

In the midst of an unexpected event, it's typical to experience fear, concern, and an overall feeling of being out of control. No one likes to feel this way. Those who have prepared can react quickly rather than sit in a state of shock. In any event, we don't simply want to survive, we want to thrive, and those who prepare for emergencies—mentally, physically, and spiritually—are less likely to experience negative emotions and more likely to be able to adapt.

BE PROACTIVE— PREPARE BEFOREHAND

FEMA—the Federal Emergency Management Agency—and other preparedness organizations suggest that every family have a two-week supply of food, water, and other necessities, in case roads are blocked and supplies can't get through. We witnessed the need for this after Hurricane Katrina in 2005, when the impact on the community was devastating.

Learning from past mistakes can be the best way not to repeat history. Having a supply of food and other emergency items can give your family a cushion to fall upon. We know that accidents and unforeseen circumstances can happen; why not prepare for them and be ahead of the game?

It's my hope that this book will show you that thriving in the midst of a personal or widespread disaster is an achievable goal. Understanding what types of foods to keep in your pantry for the best overall health and nutrition, and having an array of recipes on hand

for using them, will help keep you thriving.

Like the ancestors who came before us, we are people who will bind together to help those we care for. But we have to start by preparing for our own family's needs.

THE ECONOMICS OF PREPPING

Many believe that stocking preparedness items is just too pricey for their family budgets. But let's be honest with ourselves—can we afford an extra $5 per grocery-shopping trip? By adding a few items to your cart each time, you can create a solid preparedness pantry. A benefit of this approach is that you won't have to buy everything at once.

People often bemoan the fact that they can barely afford groceries for the week, let alone supplies for an impending disaster. Considering the whole thing out of reach, they load their carts with perishable foods and resign themselves to the belief that preparation is out of reach. It's time for a new mindset! Prepping and stockpiling can actually be your economic salvation. Here are a few reasons why:

- As you watch the price of food increase weekly, you can feel secure in the fact that you've paid less for your goods.
- Preps are investments that you can use right now.

- When times get tough, you won't have to worry about going hungry—you have a full supply of ingredients close at hand.
- After a month of purchasing for your stockpile, you'll shop to replenish supplies instead of being victim to the "just-in-time" grocery-shopping mentality.

STOCKPILE TO FIGHT INFLATION

Every trip to the grocery store brings a new awareness of the inflation hitting the world economy. The U.S. Consumer Price Index reports an increase of nearly 6% in 2011, with another 4% expected for 2012. That's nearly a 10% increase! Let's do the math, based on a weekly grocery bill of $100 in 2011.

$100 x 0.10 = $10

That means you'd pay an additional $10 for the same amount of food. That doesn't sound like much, right? Now let's multiply that by 52 weeks:

$10 x 52 = $520

That $520 is a whole lot more, isn't it? In 2011, your money would have bought another five-week supply of food!

Stockpiling can help you fight inflation by allowing you to pay the lowest possible price for foods that you commonly eat.

BEAT THE GROCERY STORES AT THEIR OWN GAME

Grocery stores play a weekly shell game with customers. They advertise a loss-leader item, such as a jar of spaghetti sauce for $1. Consumers are excited, because that same jar of sauce is normally $3. They don't notice that the pasta they buy to go with the sauce has been marked up by 33% to allow for profit. Have you ever gone to the store and discovered that your child's favorite breakfast cereal has gone from $3.99 a box to $5.99 in a week? This is the grocery industry in action—getting the consumer to pay whatever's asked by adjusting prices constantly.

You can beat them at this game by starting a price book. If you have your grocery receipts from the last few weeks, that will give you a starting point; otherwise, scour the sales flyers. For each item you normally buy, write down the best price you can find. This is your baseline, which you can adjust up or down as time goes on. For example:

Spaghetti sauce (can)—$.89
Lean ground beef—$2.99 per pound
Spaghetti—$1.19

The following week, check the flyers again. And look—now spaghetti is on sale! Compare these prices:

Spaghetti sauce (can)—$1.29
Lean ground beef—$2.99 per
 pound
Spaghetti—$0.99

Notice that the price of sauce went up and the price of pasta went down. If you purchased the sauce when it was on sale and the pasta on sale this week, you've saved $.50 on your family's meal. If you could save $.50 on every supper over the course of a year, you'd save $182.50. If you could save that much for three meals a day, the number jumps to nearly $550 per year. You can buy a lot of extra food for $550!

I estimate that I save even more than that, because I now purchase only loss leaders. Look for words like these:

- Limited quantities
- Only six per family
- While supplies last

Of course, this doesn't always guarantee a good deal. Check your price book to be sure.

YOU CAN EAT YOUR PREPS

I'm about to throw you a curve ball. You can use your preparedness food supply without being in a disaster situation. In fact, if you aren't eating your stockpiled food, you're doing it wrong!

Anyone involved in prepping has heard the adage, "Store what you eat and eat what you store." Truer words have never been spoken.

Purchase items your family normally enjoys for your stockpile. If you invest in a dozen #10 cans of freeze-dried whatchamacallits and then discover you really hate freeze-dried whatchamacallits, you've just wasted a lot of money, and valuable storage space.

Think about the menu you've served your family over the past weeks. Write down what you normally have for breakfast, pack in school lunches, and eat for dinner. These are what you should look for great deals on. In fact, many of your favorite perishable items can be dehydrated or canned for future use. And any of the recipes in this book can be made with dehydrated, canned, or freeze-dried foods.

If you buy a dozen cans of tuna on sale, whip up some tuna salad for school lunches. Make a tuna noodle casserole for supper! Don't just stick those cans of tuna in the back of your pantry to be used only in case of emergency.

PREPPING FOR ECONOMIC DISASTERS

The most common disaster facing families these days is that of economic downturn and job loss. If your income is lost or decreased dramatically, the stockpile in your pantry will become worth its weight in gold. You'll be able to get by without purchasing groceries for a few weeks out of the month, making your money stretch a lot further. The neighbor without a stockpile, on the other hand, will still be a slave to weekly grocery shopping. A good stockpile allows you to easily transition into crisis mode and drop your food spending to less than $20 per week. In difficult economic times, that can be what helps you make your mortgage payment, keep the electricity turned on, or keep your growing children in warm clothes.

JUST-IN-TIME SHOPPING

Most of us have fallen into the habit of shopping the same way grocery stores stock their shelves. It's called the "just-in-time" concept. Grocery stores get two to five shipments of food each day. If something causes a breakdown in the transportation grid, they could run out of many items in as few as two or three days—assuming frantic customers don't clear the shelves before that.

It's not uncommon for consumers to buy groceries in the same way. If you don't shop ahead, you're a hostage to price fluctuations when you're out of something. But once you've built a basic stockpile, that's no longer the case. By keeping track of what you have, what you need, and how much you're willing to pay, you can consistently get the best prices—and you'll rarely run out of anything.

You can graduate from weekly grocery shopping to "replenishing." If pasta is expensive this week but rice is on sale, only buy rice. You still have three packages of pasta sitting on your shelves, so there's no urgency to buy an overpriced item.

YOU CAN'T AFFORD NOT TO STOCK UP!

Take a look at your grocery budget. Whatever you normally spend, try to take at least 10% of that amount to start your stockpile. Make a commitment to your family to build your stockpile; this is the one investment guaranteed to yield a solid return. Here are some quick tips:

- **Buy at least one stockpile item every week**. A 1-pound bag of dried beans makes 10 to 12 adult servings. A 1-pound bag of rice also makes about 10 servings. For just a few dollars, these two ingredients could combine to make nearly a dozen meals.
- **Work cheap meals into your weekly menu.** Get out of the meat-and-potatoes mindset and add some inexpensive meals to your repertoire. If you can feed your family for $2 instead of $10, you've just saved $8 that can go toward your stockpile. Consider homemade soups,

spaghetti with marinara sauce, beans and rice, or baked potatoes.

■ **Use your leftovers.** If food that normally gets thrown away is combined into a new dish, in effect you've gotten a free meal. Save the last little bits of food and combine them in a pot pie, a soup, a stew, or a casserole.

■ **Make meat an accent instead of the main course**. For example, instead of serving ham along with scalloped potatoes, dice up some ham into a ham and potato casserole.

■ **Brew your own coffee.** Are you one of those people who hit the drive-thru every morning to get coffee before work? Spend $5 per workday and you'll end up spending a whopping $1,825 per year! If you and your spouse both indulge in this habit, you're looking at $3,650 per year.

■ **Take your lunch to work.** Eating lunch out every day is another way to take away from your stockpiling budget. The average fast-food meal costs $7; at that rate, lunches out could cost you nearly $2,000 per year. Imagine what you could add to your stockpile with that money. Your wallet, waistline, and cholesterol level will all thank you.

2 DON'T JUST SURVIVE, THRIVE!

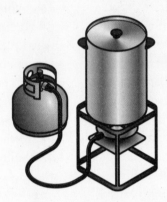

After Hurricane Katrina stopped food supply lines dead in their tracks, many hurricane victims didn't have access to food or clean water for weeks. To prevent starvation, they were given Meals Ready to Eat (MREs), and in most cases these instant meals weren't well received. Rather than depending on government organizations and emergency responders to provide you with food, why not create a versatile emergency pantry that encompasses your family's dietary preferences and needs?

Your emergency food pantry should include dry goods that you normally buy. Many favorite foods are available as "just add water" mixes, and having a supply of these will cut down on preparation time and create that sense of normality we strive for during chaotic times. Just knowing that your family has food to eat helps to bolster everyone's spirits. For example, my family loves to eat pancakes for breakfast on weekends, so we keep a good supply of the "just add water" pancake mix on hand. Not long ago a bad thunderstorm knocked out our electricity. I could tell that my children were nervous and looking to me for guidance. I made smiley-face pancakes, and we had a flashlight picnic in the living room. For the pancakes and my calm manner, I got instant smiles from the kids, and they began to relax and accept the situation. It just goes to show that smiles of any kind are infectious! (Hugs work the same way.)

GET SMART ABOUT SURVIVAL

Thriving during an emergency may mean altering your normal diet. Americans love their meat, and for many families it's a "must" for meals. But when perishables can't be kept at a constant temperature, vegetarian alternatives can help. If having meat with every meal is imperative, consider dehydrated or canned meats.

In a crisis situation, pay close attention to what you put inside your body. Dietary wellness goes beyond ensuring that your family eats its veggies. A healthy diet incorporates carbohydrates, proteins, fats, and vitamins. Your intention is to thrive, and you can't lose sight of that goal in an emergency. Without a well-rounded diet, you won't have the strength to engage in rigorous activity to benefit survival, so be sure to include healthy foods and vitamin supplements in your pantry.

Your overall health will benefit from making the substitutions shown in the following chart.

INGREDIENTS	HEALTHY SUBSTITUTES	DID YOU KNOW?
Table salt	Sea salt	Sea salt contains 84 minerals that are removed in the processing of table salt.
White sugar	Honey, molasses	Natural sugars don't cause the blood sugar crash that comes after eating refined sugar.
White flour	Whole wheat flour	Whole wheat flour still contains the bran, the most nutritious part of the wheat.
White rice	Brown rice, quinoa	As with wheat, the bran is removed to make white rice white.
Butter/oil	Herbs	Try seasoning dishes highly with herbs instead of added fats.
Whole eggs	1 tablespoon soy flour mixed with 1 tablespoon water	This is an easy low-cholesterol baking substitute (it's frugal, too!).
Oil/vegetable shortening	Applesauce	Substitute applesauce for half the oil in muffin and cake recipes to cut fat and cholesterol. It can be used as an egg substitute, too! Simply add ¼ cup of applesauce per egg in baked goods such as muffins, pancakes, or yeast-free quick breads.
White pasta	Whole wheat pasta	Much of the fiber is lost in the processing of white pasta.

INGREDIENTS	HEALTHY SUBSTITUTES	DID YOU KNOW?
Ground beef	Organic soy crumbles/TVP (textured vegetable protein)	When making a dish with ground beef, replace half of the beef with TVP. If you're making spaghetti sauce or chili, your family won't know the difference.
Craisins	Dried cranberries	Craisins are loaded with sulphites and added sugar.
Canned beef	Freeze-dried beef or dehydrated beef pieces	You'll get all of the protein without the added chemicals.

WATER: YOUR MOST VITAL PREP

Put simply, water is more important than food.

During a natural emergency—hurricane, tornado, extreme storm, earthquake—the water supply can be interrupted for days, even weeks. Water is one of the first items to disappear off store shelves when disaster threatens. At the very least, you should have a three-day water supply consisting of 1 gallon per person per day, the amount recommended by national disaster organizations. Moreover, it would be wise to prepare for the event that the water supply isn't safe for longer periods and have a means to filter water. A normally active person needs to drink at least 2 quarts (8 cups) of water every day. Take into account that if you live in a hot environment, even more water is required especially by children, nursing mothers, and the ill. Besides drinking water, you'll need water for cleaning/sanitizing, food preparation, and pets.

STORING WATER CONTAINERS

- Keep emergency water in a cool, dark place in your home, in each of your vehicles, and at your workplace.
- Like your food, your water should be rotated to ensure freshness.
- Although bottled water can be stored indefinitely (even after the "best by" date), according to the FDA, the bottled water's appearance, smell, or taste may change somewhat, but the water will be safe to consume.
- It's possible to keep water in food-grade containers intended for water storage. Many have repurposed 1-liter soda bottles and juice bottles for this. The containers must be thoroughly washed, sanitized, and rinsed. Do not re-use plastic milk containers for storing water. Even if you try to clean them thoroughly, any leftover sugars and proteins will provide per-

fect places for bacteria to grow. FEMA advises when storing water in bottles to fill the sanitized bottle to the top with regular tap water. If the tap water has been commercially treated with chlorine, you do not need to add anything else to the water to keep it clean. If the water comes from a well or other water source that is not treated with chlorine, treat water accordingly using the following purification methods.

- Only store clean, ready-to-drink water. Tap water needs to be purified. Ask public health authorities or your water provider whether your tap water should be used and how it should be treated.
- Since gallon jugs are bulky, consider layering a three-day supply of water jugs and bottles with water treatment and storage supplies, in case of extended emergency conditions. The WaterBOB, for instance, is a food-grade plastic liner that fits in your bathtub; you can fill it with enough water to last for several days, and the liner will keep the contents fresh. Also consider investing in a water filtration system such as Katadyn or Berkey; these can ensure quality drinking water when tap or well water is questionable.

TREATING WATER

When water sources are compromised, people within a fifty-mile radius can become ill if just one person handles water or disposes of waste incorrectly. Learning how to treat water before an emergency occurs will ensure that your family doesn't fall victim. When there's any doubt about the quality of your drinking water, treat it by one of the following methods to eliminate contaminating parasites, bacteria, and viruses.

BOILING

Boiling is the easiest and safest way to treat water. Bring the water to a rolling boil for 1 full minute, keeping in mind that some of it will evaporate. (If you're more than a mile above sea level, boil for three minutes.) Let the water cool. The taste of boiled water can be improved by adding oxygen back in, which you can do by pouring the water back and forth between two clean containers.

CHEMICAL TREATMENT

If boiling water isn't possible, chemical disinfection is advised.

Bleach—Sodium hypochlorite of 5.25% to 6% concentration should be the only active ingredient in the bleach you use to treat water. There should be no added soap or fragrance. Make sure the bleach is fragrance free before using it to treat water.

1. Filter the water through a piece of cloth or a coffee filter to remove any solid particles.

2. Add 8 drops or ⅛ teaspoon of liquid chlorine bleach per gallon of cooled water. Ensure that your bleach bottles are within their expiration date. Bleach expires after one year and loses its effectiveness. Stir to mix, then let stand for 30 minutes.

IODINE TABLETS—Follow the manufacturer's instructions. Iodine must be stored in a dark container, since sunlight will inactivate the tablets.

Be aware that some people are allergic to iodine and cannot use this form of water purification. Persons who have thyroid problems or are on lithium, women over age 50, and pregnant women should consult their physician prior to using iodine for purification. Also, some people who are allergic to shellfish are also allergic to iodine.

CHLORINE GRANULES (Calcium Hypochlorite)—Chlorine granules can be used by those who have iodine allergies or restrictions. An advantage of storing chlorine granules is the shelf life is much longer compared to bleach. To make a bleach solution using chlorine, add one teaspoon of chlorine granules per 2 gallons of water. To disinfect water, add 2½ teaspoons of the solution to 1 gallon of water.

Ensure that when storing granular chlorine, it is kept in its original container and stored in a cool, dry place that is not located near any flammable objects.

Try this camping trick: if you add a vitamin C tablet to chlorine-treated water, the chlorine taste vanishes. Make sure the purification process is complete before you add the vitamin C.

MICROPUR TABLETS—According to the maker of these tablets, Katadyn, this is the only disinfection system effective against viruses, bacteria, cryptosporidium, and giardia. One tablet is used per 1 quart of water; follow the manufacturer's instructions. The tablets leave no residual chemical taste.

HIDDEN WATER SOURCES

Look beyond the faucet to find "secret" water supplies in your home. Consider these possibilities:

- Melted ice cubes
- Liquids from canned goods, such as fruits or vegetables
- Water drained from pipes[1]—To use, let air into the plumbing by turning on the faucet at the highest level in your home. A small amount of water will trickle out. Then drain water from the lowest faucet in the home.
- Your hot-water tank[1]—Turn off the electricity or gas that powers the tank, and shut off the

1 Always treat water taken from water heaters and pipes.

water intake valve to keep contaminated water from flowing
in. Let the water in the heater
cool. Open the drain valve at the
bottom of the tank and place
a clean container underneath.
Start the water flowing by turning on one of the hot water
faucets in your home. Be sure to
refill the tank before the electricity or gas is turned back on; in
the case of gas, a professional
will need to turn it on.

- Toilet tank—The water in the
tank (not the bowl) is safe to
drink unless chemical treat-
ments have been added.

WHAT FOODS SHOULD I STORE?

To be nutrition-ready for extended
emergencies, you need to store the
right types of foods. Keep carbohydrates, proteins, fats, and vitamins
in mind when planning your food
pantry to give you the best bang for
your buck as far as nutrition goes.

- **Carbohydrates**. Carbohydrates
  provide the body with energy.
  They have a symbiotic relation-
  ship with proteins by protect-
  ing the protein stores in the
  body. The American College
  of Sports Medicine suggests
  that between 45% and 65% of
  your daily calories should come
  from carbs. The best carbs are
  complex and come from natural
  sources containing fiber, such
  as fresh vegetables, fruits, whole
  grains, and low-fat milk.
- **Protein.** Protein will help your
  body repair cells and rebuild
  muscles. It is recommended
  that 15% of daily calories come
  from protein.
- **Beans**. An excellent emergency
  storage food—become a complete protein when accompanied
  by a grain such as rice or quinoa.
- **Fats**. As much as we might like
  to eliminate fats from our diets,
  they play a vital role in maintaining healthy skin and hair,
  insulating body organs against
  shock, maintaining body temperature, and promoting healthy
  cell function. Fats also serve as
  an energy store for the body.
  A 2,000 calorie per day diet
  should include 67 grams of fat
  per day.
- **Vitamins and minerals**. Vitamins
  protect against infection and
  disease, help the body grow,
  assist in metabolism, and facili-
  tate the removal of waste. For a
  regular diet, it's recommended
  that we get our vitamins by eating fresh fruits and vegetables;
  however, it doesn't hurt to take a
  multivitamin daily.

WHICH ARE MOST IMPORTANT?	WHY DO YOU NEED THEM?	WHERE CAN YOU FIND THEM NATURALLY?
Vitamin A	Helps with vision, the immune system, major organ functioning, growth, and reproduction.	Dairy products, animal fat, carrots, and leafy green vegetables. Dandelions are full of vitamin A, and the green leaves are packed with other vitamins and nutrients, including calcium.
Vitamin B Complex	Needed for the nervous system, healthy skin, healthy energy levels, cell production, digestion, respiration, and bone marrow production. Helps metabolism, regulates hormone production, and protects the body from free-radical damage.	All meats, green plants (vegetables), dairy products, grains, and cereals. Try dandelions, chicory, or banana leaf, pine nuts, walnuts, and perhaps even wild grains or rice.
Vitamin C	Builds healthy skin, bones, tissues, and tendons and assists in absorbing iron. Essential for healthy teeth and gums and for healing wounds or fractures. Protects the body from free-radical damage.	Fresh fruits and vegetables. Citrus fruits, tomatoes, and broccoli have high levels of vitamin C. Rosehips are extremely high in vitamin C. The needles on pine boughs can be brewed to make a tea—not that tasty, but it does provide vitamin C.
Vitamin D	Helps maintain the immune system. Regulates the absorption of phosphorus and calcium in the body.	Eggs, dairy products, and fish with fatty flesh (tuna, salmon, sardines, and oysters).
Vitamin E	Protects the body from free-radical damage. Contributes to immune system functioning.	Rice and green leafy vegetables.
Vitamin K	Assists in blood clotting.	Produced naturally by our intestinal tract and present in soybean, olive, and canola oils, broccoli, watercress, spinach, egg yolks, leafy green plants, wild chicory, fish liver oils, and other foods.

POPULAR EMERGENCY PANTRY FOODS

When you make a list of foods to stockpile, keep these basic principles in mind:

- Emergency food shouldn't need refrigeration, and it should require little electricity or fuel to prepare.
- The food should be versatile and have a long shelf life.
- It should provide nutrition and should contain little salt.

Here's a list of the most popular food staples to stock in emergency pantries:

1. Canned fruits, vegetables, meats, and soups
2. Dried legumes (beans, lentils, etc.)

3. Crackers

4. Nuts

5. Pasta sauce

6. Peanut butter

7. Pasta

8. Flour (white, whole wheat)

9. Seasonings (vanilla, salt, pepper, paprika, cinnamon, taco seasoning, etc.)

10. Sugar

11. Bouillon cubes or granules (chicken, vegetable, beef)

12. Kitchen staples (baking soda, baking powder, yeast, vinegar)

13. Honey

14. Unsweetened cocoa powder

15. Jell-O or pudding mixes

16. Whole grains (barley, bulgur, cornmeal, couscous, oats, quinoa, rice, wheat berries)

17. Nonfat dried milk

18. Plant-based oil (corn oil, vegetable oil, coconut oil, olive oil)

19. Cereals

20. Seeds for eating and sprouting

21. Popcorn (not the microwavable kind)

22. Instant potato flakes

23. Packaged meals (macaroni and cheese, hamburger helper, ramen noodles, etc.)

24. Purified drinking water

25. Fruit juices, teas, coffee, drink mixes

When you visit the grocery store, don't limit yourself to these items. You can create a personalized preparedness pantry to suit your family's unique dietary needs and preferences. For example, I have a friend who keeps a stock of protein powder because she subscribes to a high-protein diet. She's taught me that you can add protein powder to more than just drinks. For recipes that include protein powder, see Kid-Approved (page 146)and Desserts (page 187) chapters.

HOW MUCH FOOD DO I NEED?

Figuring out how much food to store can seem overwhelming at first. The following chart can help you calculate how much of certain foods you need to weather a thirty-day disaster. (Canned goods aren't included.) The following amounts would meet the needs of two adults for a month:

LEGUMES		SUGARS	
Lima Beans	0.83 lbs	Honey	0.50 lbs
Soy Beans	1.67 lbs	Sugar	6.67 lbs
Split Peas	0.83 lbs	Brown Sugar	0.50 lbs
Lentils	0.83 lbs	Molasses	0.17 lbs
Dry Soup Mix	0.83 lbs	Corn Syrup	0.50 lbs
Dry Beans (mix)	5.00 lbs	Jams	0.50 lbs
Total Legumes	10.00 lbs	Flavored Gelatin	0.17 lbs
		Fruit Drink Mix	1.00 lbs
GRAINS		Total Sugars	10.00 lbs
Wheat	25.00 lbs		
Flour	4.17 lbs	KITCHEN ESSENTIALS	
Cornmeal	4.17 lbs	Baking Powder	0.17 lbs
Oats	4.17 lbs	Baking Soda	0.17 lbs
Rice	8.33 lbs	Yeast	0.08 lbs
Pasta	4.17 lbs	Salt	0.83 lbs
Total Grains	50.01 lbs	Vinegar	0.08 gal
FATS AND OILS		DAIRY	
Shortening	0.67 lbs	Dry Milk	10.00 lbs
Vegetable Oil	0.33 gal	Evaporated Milk	2.0 cans
Mayonnaise	0.33 qts	Other	2.17 lbs
Salad Dressing	0.17 qts	Total Dairy	16.17 lbs
Peanut Butter	0.67 lbs		
Total Fats	2.17 lbs		

Here's what a family of two adults and three children would need for a month:

LEGUMES		SUGARS	
Lima Beans	1.08 lbs	Honey	0.75 lbs
Soy Beans	2.92 lbs	Sugar	11.67 lbs
Split Peas	1.08 lbs	Brown Sugar	0.75 lbs
Lentils	1.08 lbs	Molasses	0.42 lbs
Dry Soup Mix	1.08 lbs	Corn Syrup	0.75 lbs
Dry Beans (mix)	8.75 lbs	Jams	0.75 lbs
Total Legumes	16.00 lbs	Flavored Gelatin	0.42 lbs
		Fruit Drink Mix	1.75 lbs
GRAINS		Total Sugars	17.25 lbs
Wheat	43.75 lbs		
Flour	7.17 lbs	KITCHEN ESSENTIALS	
Corn Meal	7.17 lbs	Baking Powder	0.42 lbs
Oats	7.17 lbs	Baking Soda	0.42 lbs
Rice	14.58 lbs	Yeast	0.21 lbs
Pasta	7.17 lbs	Salt	1.58 lbs
Total Grains	87.01 lbs	Vinegar	0.21 gal
FATS AND OILS		DAIRY	
Shortening	1.17 lbs	Dry Milk	17.50 lbs
Vegetable Oil	0.58 gal	Evaporated Milk	3.50 can
Mayonnaise	0.58 qts	Other	3.67 lbs
Salad Dressing	0.42 qts	Total Dairy	28.17 lbs
Peanut Butter	1.17 lbs		
Total Fats	3.92 lbs		

To determine the quantities of other foods for your family, visit ReadyNutrition.com for a food storage calculator.

BE A PLANNER!

To make the most of your pre-paredness grocery list, preplan your emergency menu to ensure that you have everything you need for a varied diet. Having your meals planned out relieves a tremendous amount of stress and cuts down on food fatigue (the boredom of eating the same food repeatedly). Be sure to include special treat items for family members—and yourself. If you're having an emotional or rainy day, indulging in a treat or treating your children to something special will lift spirits and break up the monotony. Treats might be pudding, Jell-O, cheese crackers, apple-sauce, hot chocolate, popcorn, or dried fruit leathers, for example.

SPICE OF LIFE!

One way to avoid food fatigue when cooking from your storage pantry is to add herbs and spices. A trip to the bulk-foods store can get you some gourmet blends; all you'll need are a few jars in which to store them. Another option is to start your own herb garden. If you dehydrate your cut herbs, you'll have a constant supply to use in your own seasoning blends.

The following mixes can be made from dried herbs that you've purchased or that you've grown yourself and dehydrated. Some of the mixes call for salt, and although regular table salt can be used, kosher salt is recommended because its larger grains are more absorbent. That will keep your blends fresh longer. To test whether an herb or spice is still potent, rub or crush a small amount in your hand, then taste and smell it. If the aroma and flavor is weak, it should be discarded. In general, use the following guidelines to estimate the shelf lives of your spices:

- Herbs: 1 to 3 years
- Extracts: 4 years, except pure vanilla, which lasts indefinitely
- Ground Spices: 2 to 3 years
- Whole Spices: 3 to 4 years
- Seasoning Blends: 1 to 2 years

Use a spice mill or electric coffee grinder to grind these spice mixes into fine powders and then transfer them into glass jars. A pepper mill or mortar and pestle is a suitable off-grid alternative to grinding spices.

APPLE PIE SPICE MIX

¼ cup ground cinnamon

1 tablespoon ground allspice

2 teaspoons ground nutmeg

2 teaspoons ground ginger

½ teaspoon grated dried lemon zest

1 teaspoon ground cardamom (optional)

PUMPKIN PIE SPICE MIX

¼ cup ground cinnamon

2 tablespoons ground ginger

2 teaspoons ground cloves

1 teaspoon ground nutmeg

¼ teaspoon ground cardamom (optional)

CAJUN SEASONING

Add a taste of New Orleans to rice, beans, fish, or chicken with this zesty blend.

- ⅓ cup kosher salt
- ¼ cup chili powder (purchased, or from the recipe below)
- ¼ cup Hungarian paprika
- 1 tablespoon onion powder
- 1 tablespoon garlic powder
- 1 tablespoon coarsely ground black pepper
- 1 tablespoon dried basil
- 1 tablespoon dried oregano
- 1 tablespoon ground coriander
- ½ teaspoon cayenne pepper
- 2 teaspoons dried thyme
- ¼ teaspoon ground cumin
- ¼ teaspoon white pepper

CHILI POWDER

- 2 tablespoons paprika
- 2 teaspoons dried oregano
- 1½ teaspoons ground cumin
- 1¼ teaspoons garlic powder
- 1¼ teaspoons cayenne pepper
- 1 teaspoon onion powder

FRENCH HERB MIX

Try adding this mixture to soups, meats, or vegetables.

- 3 tablespoons dried marjoram
- 3 tablespoons dried thyme
- 3 tablespoons dried summer savory
- 2 tablespoons minced dried garlic

- 1 teaspoon dried basil
- 1 teaspoon dried rosemary
- 1 teaspoon dried sage
- ½ teaspoon ground fennel seeds

CHINESE FIVE-SPICE MIX

Grind the whole spices together to make this blend perfect for sprinkling into stir-fries or onto meats.

- 2 tablespoons ground anise seed or 2 whole star anise, ground
- 2 tablespoons ground fennel seed
- 2 tablespoons ground cloves
- 2 tablespoons ground peppercorns

TEX-MEX SPICE BLEND

Turn dinner into a fiesta by adding this blend to chili, taco meat, beans, or rice.

- ½ cup chili powder (purchased or made from recipe)
- ¼ cup paprika
- 1 tablespoon ground cumin
- 1½ teaspoons garlic powder
- 1 teaspoon onion powder
- 2 teaspoons dried oregano
- 2 teaspoons dried parsley
- 1 teaspoon salt

FAJITA SEASONING MIX

- 2½ tablespoons chili powder (purchased or made from recipe)
- 1 tablespoon kosher salt
- 1 tablespoon lemon pepper seasoning
- 1 tablespoon sugar
- 2½ teaspoons crushed chicken bouillon cubes or granules
- 2 teaspoons onion powder

½ teaspoon garlic powder

½ teaspoon cayenne pepper

¼ teaspoon crushed red pepper flakes

½ teaspoon ground cumin

GREEK SEASONING MIX

Flavor shish kebobs, veggies, meat, and rice with this mixture.

2 tablespoons dried oregano

4 teaspoons dried mint

4 teaspoons dried thyme

1 tablespoon dried minced garlic

2 teaspoons dried basil

2 teaspoons dried marjoram

2 teaspoons dried minced onion

HOMEMADE VEGETABLE ALL-PURPOSE SEASONING

Makes 2 cups

3 medium onions, cut into 2-inch cubes

5 celery ribs, diced

3 medium Russet potatoes, peeled and diced

3 medium red bell peppers, diced

3 large green bell peppers, diced

3 large carrots, peeled and diced

2 large parsnips, peeled and diced

8 to 10 garlic cloves

1 bunch fresh parsley

chicken bouillon granules, to taste

In a saucepan over high heat, combine diced potatoes and carrots with enough water to cover them. Cook for 5 minutes until soft. Drain.

Combine all the ingredients except the bouillon in a blender or food processor and whirl until fully processed. Place on a jelly roll tray in food dehydrator at a setting of 135°F to 145°F for 5 hours or until dried and crumbly. Once the mixture is thoroughly dried, add 1 tablespoon bouillon granules at a time to taste. Store in a jar for up to one year.

ROTATING YOUR FOOD SUPPLY

Think of your preparedness pantry as your in-home convenience store, to be used whenever you need it. In fact, incorporating your stored foods into your regular menu-planning and replenishing them as they get used up will ensure that your preparedness foods are at optimal freshness. First In First Out (FIFO) is a restaurant-business term that can be incorporated into your food storage philosophy. To get the most out of your investment, use the FIFO approach by placing items with the earliest expiration dates in front so they'll be used first.

Keeping your pantry stocked with fresh food means doing inventory checks from time to time. My family takes inventory of our supplies every six months to make sure canned goods, preserves, and other items are within their expiration dates. We also check to make sure we're not running low on any essentials. If anything is close to expiring, it's taken to the kitchen pantry to be used. Follow the FIFO strategy for both store bought and home-canned goods.

ESSENTIAL TOOLS

In an emergency, when you're likely to be without many modern conveniences, certain tools become essential. When selecting your tools, keep your lifestyle in mind. For example, if you have a baby, you'll probably need a baby food mill. Many favorite kitchen tools can be found in "hand crank" versions; look online or in homesteading magazines. You don't have to invest in top-of-the-line brands or models. I purchased my off-grid tools in the low to midprice range, and they get the job done.

FOOD DEHYDRATOR—This is probably the most used of all of my preparedness tools. Are any of you guilty of having produce or meat go bad before you get around to using it? According to a study from the University of Arizona, more than 40% of the food produced in this country doesn't get eaten (Source, UA News). That's a lot of food going to waste.

A food dehydrator can address this dilemma. After my produce sits in the fruit bowl for a week, I cut it up and dehydrate it to make a new snack for the kids, or to use in cooking. If meat hasn't been used, I cook and dehydrate it for later use. Another option is making meat jerky snacks, which don't last long in my house. Many of the recipes in this book can be made with dehydrated fruits, vegetables, and meats.

OUTDOOR GRILL—Many meals can be prepared on a gas or charcoal grill. Some of the newer types even have a side burner for pots. Have plenty of foil for packet meals, along with plastic ovenproof cooking bags for warming food in boiling water—leaving you with reusable water and no dirty pot. Keep an extra tank of propane on hand for your gas grill, or stock up on charcoal or nontoxic wood for your charcoal grill.

SUN OVEN—In the aftermath of storms or other disasters, the electricity may be off for two weeks or longer. Do you know how to cook your food without a working stove or oven? By using the sun's energy, a solar oven will cook your meals and bake tasty breads and desserts! This gadget works best when the UV index is 7 or higher and the sun is high overhead, with few clouds. The only drawback is that certain foods take longer to cook and you're dependent on full sun, but a solar cooker is definitely a good investment if you find yourself off-grid.

NON-ELECTRIC AND HAND-CRANK APPLIANCES—Did you know that there are hand-crank blenders, popcorn poppers, baby food mills, and ice-cream makers? These "off-grid" appliances can add convenience at an otherwise chaotic moment. If you can't live without that morning smoothie, put your ingredients in the blender and get an arm workout at the same time. A hand-crank blender can be used to make soup or even fresh juice to add nutrition to your diet.

WHEAT GRINDER—How lovely would it be to have fresh bread in the midst of an emergency? Wheat grinders grind wheat, as well as smaller grains and legumes, into flour. The higher-end models can be costly, but there are basic grinders that cost around $70 and work very well. I've ground wheat, legumes, and smaller grains using a lower-end grinder and have had no issues. I must admit that the more expensive grinders do the job faster and the flour comes out finer, in some cases.

SPROUTER—This will more than likely be the least expensive tool you'll purchase, but it will pay for itself many times over while helping to keep you healthy. There are different types of sprouters, ranging from basic to advanced. I have a sprouting jar lid that cost around $2, and I prefer it to some of the other sprouting tools I've purchased. Some people even wrap small seeds in moist paper towels to sprout them.

WATER PURIFICATION SYSTEMS—Having a supply of fresh drinking water is essential for thriving during an emergency. One way to cut down on water storage space is to invest in a water purification system.

WHEN DISASTER STRIKES, WHAT DO I DO?

How many times have you "popped out" to the grocery store just to grab one or two ingredients for a meal you were making? During a disaster, this luxury could disappear. If the supply trucks stop running, within a matter of days the only food available will be what you already have. And if you lose power, your perishable food could quickly become contaminated.

Food safety is vital at all times, of course, but if medical care is limited or inaccessible, food poisoning could be deadly. If you have any doubt as to whether food is safe or spoiled, throw it out—it's not worth the risk. If you're without electricity, use the following tips suggested by the Food and Drug Administration to keep your refrigerated and frozen foods safe for as long as possible.

- Limit opening the refrigerator and freezer to keep food cold for as long as possible. Refrigerated food will stay cold for four to six hours, assuming the door is left closed as much as possible. In a fully stocked freezer, foods remain safely frozen for approximately two days if the door stays closed.
- Cover the fridge or freezer with blankets to help keep the interior cold longer.
- Keep water-filled soda bottles in your freezer to help preserve perishable foods if you are without power—and when the bottles defrost, you'll have drinking water.
- Items from the freezer that have thawed can be cooked and then refrozen.
- Equip your fridge and freezer with thermometers so you can tell whether or not food is still safe to eat. If the following foods have been stored above 40°F for more than two hours, they should be discarded (source http://www.fsis.usda.gov/ Factsheets/keeping_food_Safe_ during_an_emergency/index .asp).
  - Meat, raw or cooked (including lunch meats)
  - Casseroles, stews, or soups
  - Most dairy products
  - Mayonnaise or creamy salad dressings
  - Cooked pasta, potatoes, or rice
- These foods are more stable and can last for up to two days above 40°F:
- Butter or margarine
- Hard or processed cheese
- Fresh fruits and vegetables
- Mustard, ketchup, barbecue sauce
- Olives, pickles, relishes
- Vinegar-based salad dressings
- Peanut butter
- Jams and jellies

STAYING CHILL

If a disaster threatens your food supply, you may want to consider alternative refrigeration methods. Although ice chests are the popular choice, the need for large quantities of ice poses a problem when there's no electricity. There are other possibilities to consider. Some of these may seem archaic, but they've been tested over the years and have been found to work:

- Root cellar
- Cold spring house
- Refrigerator/freezer operating on alternative fuel, such as propane
- Old icebox that holds 20-pound ice blocks (or stacked bags of ice)
- Zeer, an earthenware pot lined with wet sand, holding an inner food-storage pot

- Hole in the ground, since the ground stays around 60°F at 10 feet below the surface

BASIC SANITATION

Another challenge during a disaster is basic sanitation. It's imperative to have clean hands, cookware, food prep areas, and dishes and utensils. In a short-term disaster, disposable items are incredibly useful, partly because you don't have to use valuable clean water to wash them. These items are perfect to have on hand:
- Paper plates
- Disposable cups
- Plastic utensils
- Paper towels
- Baby wipes
- Disinfecting wipes
- Aluminum foil (to cover cookware and cooking surfaces)
- Garbage bags

If you don't have running water, clean your hands carefully with baby wipes and/or hand sanitizer after using the restroom, changing diapers, or dealing with garbage. Sanitation-related illnesses often occur because of poor hygiene. Take care not to cause cross-contamination when preparing food. Surfaces that have been in contact with raw meat must be cleaned immediately and sanitized before other food is prepared there. Wash your hands after touching raw meat.

In a longer-term emergency, cleaning supplies may run low. Stock a big supply of basics such as white vinegar, baking soda, and lemon juice.

FOOD RATIONING PRACTICALITIES

When the effects of a disaster are long lasting, you must wisely ration your food to ensure that your family is fed for as long as possible. If the issue includes a power outage, always use or preserve the items from your refrigerator first.

Practical considerations must be taken into account when rationing food. Although any parent feels the need to give as much of the food as possible to the children, this is not always the wisest course. The person who does the most physical activity requires the highest caloric intake. If Dad is out chopping wood and hunting all day, he must be persuaded to eat enough that he'll be able to continue these tasks successfully.

If you still have a heat source for cooking, a proactive step would be to begin preserving your perishable foods while you have access to energy.

Once you've passed the safety point of your fresh foods, it's time to assess your situation. Is this outage or break in supplies likely to be long-term? If so, you need to take steps to make the food you have last until you can harvest more food; depending on the season, you could be a year away from a fresh harvest. This is where those food preservation tools will come in handy.

MAKING MEALS STRETCH

A wise home economist can put together a meal out of thin air when other people would say, "There's nothing to eat."

Making do with fewer ingredients while wanting meals to be as filling as ever is quite a conundrum. My grandmother once told me that her mother always had a soup on the stove. The ingredients were usually leftovers, and if she was told that company was coming, she'd add water and throw in some potatoes or beans to thicken the soup.

Making the most of your food pantry is all about your mindset. Learning how to stretch food supplies helps to create a frugal lifestyle and allows us to make the most of our food investments.

Inexpensive additions can go a long way to making the most of a meal. Here are six easy ways to make meals more filling:

1. **FIBER**—Fiber-rich food sources such as beans and lentils are ideal to have in your food supply. Beans are the quintessential prepper food—cheap, nutritious, easy to store, and extremely filling. Throwing a half-cup of beans into a soup or casserole, or cooking them as a side dish, definitely fills up those hungry bellies.

2. **WHOLE GRAINS**—Grains are the basis of many pantries because of their fiber and protein content. Whole grains are popular sources of fiber, having much greater amounts of nutrients, soluble fiber, and protein than refined grains such as white bread. Whole grains can be ground into flour or used to add texture to dishes, such as if they are made into dumplings and added to a soup or stew. Wheat berries in particular are great for longer-term storage. If stored properly and in the right environment, wheat berries can last a lifetime.

3. **BREAD AND PASTA**—The starches from some "white foods" will bring some sustenance and keep morale up during an extended emergency. Simply adding a slice of bread or sprinkling in breadcrumbs will instantly thicken a soup and make it more filling. Even the water used for cooking pasta can be re-used as a soup thickener, thanks to the starch in the water.

4. **NUTS**—Almonds especially are rich in monounsaturated fatty acids and protein. Just one handful of almonds will keep

EXPANDING YOUR CANNED GOODS

Stir some inexpensive additions into canned goods to increase the number of servings in that humble can. For example:

Beef stew—Add 1 can mixed veggies and 2 cups cooked barley.

Beef stew—Add 1 cup water and a packet of gravy mix; serve over cooked egg noodles.

Chili mac—Add ½ cup processed cheese spread and 2 cups cooked macaroni.

Chili—Add 1 can kidney or black beans and 2 to 3 cups cooked rice.

Chili—Add 1 cup reconstituted TVP, 1 can diced tomatoes, and 1 can black beans.

Chili—Add 2 prepared packages macaroni and cheese.

Chicken broth—Add 2 cups water and 1 bouillon cube; make homemade dumplings in the broth.

Baked beans in tomato sauce—Add 1 can flaked ham, ¼ cup barbecue sauce, and 2 cups cooked barley.

Baked beans in tomato sauce—Add to cooked rice along with 1 can condensed tomato soup, 1 cup water, and 2 teaspoons Cajun seasoning.

Diced tomatoes—Add 3 cups cooked elbow macaroni, garlic powder, onion powder, salt, and pepper to taste.

Chicken noodle soup—Stir in 1 can peas, 1 can condensed cream of mushroom soup, and 2 cups noodles cooked in bouillon.

Condensed vegetable soup—Stir into 3 cups cooked rice or barley for a tasty pilaf.

Creamed corn—Stir in 1 package instant potato flakes, 2 tablespoons nonfat dry milk, and 4 cups water to make a thick corn chowder.

Sloppy Joe sauce—If you're serving this with ½ pound ground beef, use 2 cups dehydrated beef crumbles, rehydrated, TVP in place of half the beef; add 1 can pinto beans and 1½ teaspoons chili powder.

Spaghetti sauce—Add 1 can diced tomatoes and 1 can white kidney beans; stir into cooked spaghetti, sparingly covering the pasta.

Spaghetti sauce—Add 4 cups water, 1 can white kidney beans, 1 can spinach, and cooked pasta or rice for a mock-escarole soup.

Potato soup—Add 1 packet instant potato flakes and 4 cups water.

you full for a long time. Don't limit your nut selections to just almonds, though; any nut will do. Nuts can also be ground into flour or included in a main dish or salad to add flavor and crunch. I love adding almonds to my rice dishes.

5. **TRIMMINGS**—Freeze vegetable and meat trimmings to use for making broths and stocks. Toss peeled veggies or leftover meat parts into labeled freezer bags.

When you're ready to use them, cover these trimmings with water and simmer on low for an hour or two to make a delicious soup or stew.

"Leftover Stew or Chowder" is just what it sounds like—a marriage of leftovers that might normally be thrown out. Designate a large plastic freezer container and dump in all the tiny bits of leftovers you might previously have considered "not enough to keep." When the container is full, add water and a couple of bouillon cubes and see what you come up with. During lean times, my family has created some surprisingly tasty concoctions.

Another way of prolonging this type of meal is to dehydrate it; dehydrate the broth as you would fruit leather (see page 76) and dry the vegetables on a separate tray.

IT ALL STARTS WITH A LIST

I don't know about you, but I'm a "list person." I simply cannot operate without my lists. They keep me organized and on task, and they keep me from purchasing extraneous items.

If you're just starting out, I recommend developing a month's menu plan and purchasing the food to fulfill it. Once you've acquired a full month's food supply, you can add on and shoot for a three-

month supply, a six-month supply, and so forth.

Determine how many people you'll be feeding. Will others be joining you in an emergency situation? Some people prep for their extended family as well as immediate family members.

Creating a list of everything you need for your basic food pantry will help you keep your family's dietary needs in mind when you go shopping. A few things to consider:

- Keep things affordable. Keep a price book (see page 8) so that you'll know when to stock up on various foods.
- Look for foods that don't require electricity (refrigeration or freezing) for storage.
- Keep tabs on how much food you have in various nutrient groups: protein, fruits, vegetables, grains, and dairy.
- If there's a power outage, do you have an alternate way to cook food? Is there a way to at least boil water? If not, are you prepared with food that doesn't require heating?

THE BASIC MEAL-BY-MEAL STOCKPILE

The most basic way to stockpile, a meal-by-meal plan is utilitarian and will cover your family basic nutritional and caloric needs. It won't be gourmet, but it's a starting point to give you a month's worth of food. Many people like to start here and then expand to tastier meals offering greater variety.

Let's break this down meal by meal. Our sample family will consist of two adults and two children.

BREAKFASTS—Keep in mind that every time you cook, you're using valuable fuel. Unless you are running a woodstove constantly in wintertime, you may want to limit actual cooking to once per day.

For breakfasts, cold cereal is a quick, high-energy option that doesn't require cooking. Top your cereal with reconstituted nonfat milk and dried fruit for a well-balanced breakfast.

Based on a 1-cup serving for children and a 1½-cup serving for adults, we're looking at 5 cups of cereal per day for our family of four, or 150 cups for a 30-day month. A box of cornflakes (18 ounces) contains about 18 cups of cereal, so it would provide three days of breakfasts for all four family members, plus two additional adult servings. To feed our theoretical family for a month, we'd need eight boxes of cereal.

You can perform the same calculations for nonfat dry milk and dried fruit servings.

LUNCHES—Depending on the time of year, a piping-hot cup of soup or pasta can make for a comforting lunch. Served with crackers and a drink, this inexpensive option is easy to stock for. Condensed soups

take up little space, and if you have the facilities for boiling water, they can be heated quickly. Canned pasta, such as ravioli, also requires nothing more than a way to heat it. In a pinch, it can be eaten at room temperature.

Two cans of condensed soup per lunch would keep the edge off hunger for our hypothetical family of four, especially if it's served with crackers or over leftover rice from the previous night's meal. That means that 60 cans of soup, plus crackers, would be a basic lunchtime stockpile.

DINNERS—For dinner, most people like a sit-down meal that's a bit more elaborate than lunch and breakfast. This is entirely dependent on your cooking facilities. An excellent way to prep for dinners for a basic one-month stockpile is to select seven recipes that you'll be able to prepare, given your facilities, and simply buy four times the ingredients needed for each recipe. Browse through the recipes in this book, try out some of them, and shop for what you need to make your favorites.

MEALS FOR THE WEEK

Use this chart to list meals you plan on preparing in an emergency.

	BREAKFAST	LUNCH	DINNER
MONDAY			
TUESDAY			
WEDNESDAY			

THURSDAY			
FRIDAY			
SATURDAY			
SUNDAY			

FOOD STORAGE 101

Storing food for short- and long-term emergencies is not without its challenges. Over time, moisture, sunlight, oxygen, temperature fluctuations, and bug infestations can compromise your food supply. When this occurs, food may lose essential nutrients or be tainted and need to be thrown out—along with your monetary investment. One way to keep the enemies of food at bay is to repack your purchased dry goods in higher-quality packaging.

Most of the dry goods we buy has packaging designed for short-term use. Clear and flimsy plastic packaging can't stand up to long-term storage; it's easily punctured and is no match for the elements or hungry bugs. We need to repackage our food in higher-quality containers. Plastic 5-gallon pails, Mylar liner bags, oxygen absorbers, and desiccant pouches create additional layers of protection.

According to the United States Food and Drug Administration, certain "defects" in our food supply are unavoidable. Bugs and their eggs are on that list. But taking steps to destroy them before you repackage food can extend its shelf life. There are three methods you can use:

1. Freeze-dry goods for 72 hours.
2. Heat food in a 170°F oven for 15 to 20 minutes.
3. Add diatomaceous earth, the fossilized remains of a type of algae. Organic and safe to use on food, it kills bugs. Be sure to purchase food-grade diatomaceous earth, and add 1 cup to every 25 pounds of food. Sprinkle the bottom of the container with food-grade diatomaceous earth. Add 3 to 4 inches of dry food. Using a sifter or metal colander, sprinkle another layer of diatomaceous earth. Repeat until all the dry food is treated. Sprinkle a final light layer of diatomaceous earth on the top, then seal.

Many of the following food storage products can be purchased at preparedness stores geared toward long-term food storage such as www.PrepperPackaging.com. This website carries Mylar bags, oxygen absorbers, desiccant packets, and many other essential items.

PLASTIC CONTAINERS

Any food that you plan to keep indefinitely should be stored in food-grade plastic. Such containers won't transfer any non-food chemicals into the food, nor do they contain any chemicals that are hazardous to humans. Typically a food-grade container has a "#2" with the recycle symbol or the high-density polyethylene (HDPE) stamp on the bottom and is 75 milliliters thick. Clean containers with soapy water, rinse, and dry thoroughly. Five-gallon plastic containers are the most popular for storing food in bulk.

Make sure that your containers have airtight and spillproof lids. Lids with gaskets and gamma lids are great, as they can be opened with a simple twist of the wrist. These are typically a little more expensive than the traditional bucket lid, but they're easier to open and close—and worth every penny.

FOOD LINERS

Research has shown that small amounts of oxygen seep through the walls of plastic containers. Consequently, natural elements and even insects can find a way in. Adding a food liner such as a 5-milliliter Mylar bag will provide extra protection. Thick Mylar bags have a middle layer of aluminum and two different plastic layers on the inside and outside, making them ideal for long-term food storage. Further, Mylar bags make for a good investment because they can last up to 20 years if properly cared for, are reusable, and make

a big difference in the taste of stored food.

OXYGEN ABSORBERS AND DESICCANTS

Oxygen absorbers can greatly prolong the shelf life of stored food by inhibiting the growth of aerobic pathogens and molds. If you live in an area prone to high humidity, you may also want to consider adding desiccant packets to your food storage.

OXYGEN ABSORBERS—Oxygen absorbers come in vacuum-sealed packs and begin working the moment they're exposed to oxygen, so it's best to work as efficiently as possible.

To determine how many cubic centimeters your oxygen absorber should be, it's important to consider the type of food being packed. Requirements vary depending on the volume of the food, the "void space" (the space between food particles), and the "headspace" (the container space not filled with food). For example, if you fill a 5-gallon bucket all the way to the top with marbles, leaving no headspace, the void space is the amount of air between marbles. Because marbles don't pack as densely as, say, salt, your bucket will require a larger oxygen absorber than a 5-gallon bucket of salt.

This is the general formula for the cubic centimeters of oxygen absorption required:

Container volume
− Food volume
_____
= Residual air volume

Residual air volume
x 0.21 (because air is 21% oxygen)
_____
= Oxygen absorber size requirement

You want your oxygen absorber to meet or exceed the residual air volume in the packed container. Here's how it works. To pack 35 pounds of rice in a 5-gallon bucket, an online calculator tells us that 35 pounds of rice is equivalent to 15,875 grams (or cubic centimeters). Our 5-gallon bucket is equivalent to 18,942 cubic centimeters of air volume. Assuming the rice fills the bucket to the top, leaving no headspace, we can calculate the void space (oxygen absorber size requirement) as follows:

18,942 cc (container volume)
− 15,875 cc (food volume)
_____
= 3,067 cc (residual air volume)

3,067 (residual air volume)
X 0.21 (oxygen)
_____
= 644 cc (oxygen absorber size requirement)

NOTE: Use an online calculator, such as www.metric-conversions.org, to convert pounds to grams; 1 gram is equal to 1 cubic centimeter.

The following chart is a guide to the oxygen absorber sizes you're likely to need for some food you'll be packing. The chart assumes that containers are full and that as much air as possible has been removed. (Vacuum sealing is recommended when possible.) Oxygen absorbers are typically sold in 50, 100, 300, 500, 1,000, and 1,500-cc sizes. Since headspace and void space can't be calculated exactly, when in doubt it's best to err on the side of caution and use a larger size, as has been done for this chart.

OXYGEN ABSORBER SIZE REQUIREMENTS

	1-QUART POUCH (8" x 8")— 947 CCs	#10 CAN (0.82 gallon)— 3,910 CCs	5-GALLON BUCKET— 18,942 CCs	6-GALLON BUCKET— 22,730 CCs
Flour, pancake mix, fine powders	50–100 cc	200–300 cc	750 cc	1,000 cc
Sugar, salt, dry milk	50–100 cc	200–300 cc	750 cc	1,000 cc
Rice, grains (wheat berries, oats, etc.)	50–100 cc	200–300 cc	750–1,000 cc	1,000–1,500 cc
Dried beans	100–150 cc	300–500 cc	1,000 cc	1,500 cc
Pasta	100–200 cc	300–600 cc	1,000–1,500 cc	1,500–2,000 cc

Desiccants—Desiccant packets only moderate the moisture levels in food containers; they don't completely absorb the moisture. Desiccants shouldn't be added to flour, sugar, and salt; these ingredients need a certain amount of moisture to stay activated, and if desiccant is added, they'll turn into hard bricks.

Desiccant manufactures recommend adding two 1-ounce packets per 5 or 6-gallon pail or large barrier bag. Make sure the desiccant packets aren't touching oxygen absorbers.

Desiccant is not edible—if the packet somehow breaks open and spills onto the stored food, the entire contents of the container must be thrown away.

THE SEALING PROCESS

1. Place a Mylar bag in the plastic container. The Mylar bag should be fitted for the size of container you are using. For example, if you are using a 5-gallon plastic bucket, you will want to use an 18 x 28-inch or a 20 x 30-inch Mylar bag.
2. Add oxygen absorbers and/or desiccant in the bottom of the bag. (You'll add another oxygen absorber at the top.)
3. Begin pouring food into the Mylar bag. When the bag is about half full, shake it to make sure the food gets into all the crevices of the bag.
4. Continue adding food into the Mylar bag until the bag is ¾ full. Add another oxygen absorber on the top of the contents.
5. Begin folding the Mylar down to let any trapped air escape.
6. Seal the Mylar, using a heat clamp or an iron on its highest setting. If you use an iron, work on a hard surface, moving slowly and gently to keep from damaging the bag.

Seal across the bag in a straight line, leaving the last 2 or 3 inches unsealed.

7. Push out the last remaining trapped air, then finish sealing the bag.

8. Push the sealed Mylar bag into the plastic storage container. If you wish, add another oxygen absorber on top of the sealed bag. Place the lid securely on the container.

9. Place in a dark storage area where temperature, moisture level, and sunlight don't fluctuate.

DRY ICE ALTERNATIVE—This is another method used for food preservation. Many preppers use dry ice with Mylar bags and plastic containers, and some preppers only use the plastic food-grade containers. Dry ice can be purchased at many grocery stores, ice cream stores, and even welding stores. What makes this storage method popular is that it's very economical: a 5-pound bag of dry ice costs just $5. Dry ice is very cold, so if you use this method, use gloves when handling, and ensure that you work in a ventilated area. Also, if you're using oxygen absorbers, there is no need to use the dry ice method. Use 3 to 4 ounces of dry ice per 5-gallon bucket. This storage method can be done two different ways:

ICE ON TOP:

1. Spread a single layer of nonconductive (insulating) material such as kraft paper or foil over the contents of a nearly filled 5-gallon container. Place 4 ounces of dry ice on top.

2. Leave part of the lid unsealed until the dry ice completely evaporates (sublimates).

3. Check every 30 minutes to see if the dry ice has completely evaporated. If not, keep checking every 5 minutes.

4. When the dry ice has evaporated, remove the insulating material and seal the container.

Tip: If the sealed lids begin to bulge up, then you have sealed them prematurely. If this happens, use a bucket lid remover to crack open the lid on one side to let the excess gas escape, then seal the lid back down.

ICE ON BOTTOM:

Place 4 ounces of dry ice in the bottom of a 5-gallon storage container. Cover with nonconductive (insulating) material, such as kraft paper or foil. Add the food. Press the lid down lightly, allowing air to escape. Continue as for the on-top method.

BUILDING YOUR PANTRY

Building your food stockpile can seem overwhelming, but you might be surprised at how much you've already accomplished without even realizing it. An inventory of your cupboards can help you to realize how far you've already come.

The best way to see what you have is to bring it all out in the open and take inventory. (This might also be a great time to do some "spring cleaning" of your cabinets.) Use your countertops and kitchen table to organize, sort, and count what you have.

Sort things into groups. Your categories might include the following:

- Canned meats (tuna, chicken, Spam, dinner ham)
- Canned soups
- Canned dinners (beef stew, chili, Beefaroni)
- Canned beans
- Canned vegetables
- Canned fruit
- Jelly and jam
- Peanut butter
- Baking supplies (flour, yeast, baking soda, etc.)
- Desserts (gelatin, pudding mix)
- Boxed meals (Hamburger Helper, macaroni and cheese)
- Packaged side dishes (scalloped potatoes, flavored rice or pasta, sauce packets)
- Cereal (dry breakfast cereal, oatmeal, cream of wheat)
- Dried legumes (kidney beans, split peas, etc.)
- Dried fruit
- Sweeteners (honey, sugar, maple syrup, stevia)
- Pancake mix
- Baking mixes (cake mix, cookie mix)
- Crackers
- Canned tomato products (spaghetti sauce, tomato paste, diced tomatoes)
- Herbs and spices

Once you have everything out and organized, I bet you'll be surprised by how much you have. This, my friend, is the start of your survival pantry! Your next step is to identify how many servings of the different foods you have. Grab a pen, a notebook, and a calculator (unless you're a big fan of doing math in your head).

Use the following table to calculate the servings in some of your food packages.

SERVING SIZE	FOOD TYPE	SERVINGS PER WEIGHT
1 cup	Beans, dried	10 per 1 pound
1 cup	Rice	12 per 1 pound
1 cup	Pasta	8 per 1-pound bag
1 cup	Condensed soup	2 per 10.7-ounce can
½ cup	Canned veggies	3 per 15-ounce can

Look for serving information on the packages of other items. Once you know how many servings of various items you have, plug the numbers into an online food storage calculator like the one found at the Ready Nutrition website (readynutrition.com/resources/category/preparedness/calculators/).

You'll be able to see how long your family could sustain itself on the food you already have, and you'll be able to see where your weak points are. You may have enough pasta to last for six months because you recently hit a sale, but only enough canned fruit for a couple of weeks. Or you may have a month's supply of canned fish and meat but only a two-week supply of powdered milk. Now it's time to build on what you have.

CREATING A MASTER LIST

The best way to keep track of your preps is with a master inventory list. My family has an alphabetized list that includes everything. Here are some suggestions for creating your own master list:

- Use a computer spreadsheet program to organize and categorize your preps.
- List everything! Nothing should be excluded from your inventory.
- Alphabetizing your food categories and listing where everything is stored can be helpful when you're in a pinch.
- Store your master list in a binder that also contains emergency procedures (including evacuation routes), pertinent phone numbers, and other useful information.

WHERE TO STORE FOOD?

Ideal temperatures for food storage are between 60°F and 75°F. To ensure that the area where your food is stored is at the proper temperature and moisture level, install an indoor thermometer and hygrometer or humidity gauge. Food is best stored in relatively low humidity levels; 15% humidity or less is ideal, although ideal conditions are not always practical. Hygrometers and thermometers are available at most hardware or home-improvement stores and are relatively inexpensive.

Make sure that your food storage area is clean, free of trash, and protected from insects and the elements. Keep containers from touching walls to allow constant air circulation. Also, avoid storing food containers directly on concrete or dirt floors. Use shelving, pallets, boards, or blocks to raise the food storage above ground level.

Here are a few ideas of where you can safely store your emergency food supply:

KITCHEN PANTRY—Your kitchen pantry is the go-to place for your cooking needs, and it should continue to be so. When the food is used up here, it can be replenished with items from your emergency stores.

COLD CELLAR—Root cellars date back to prehistoric times, and cellaring remains one of the best ways to maintain the freshness and nutritional value of some foods. A root cellar is a simple way to preserve food without processing it or using any electricity or fuel. An underground storage space provides the right temperature and humidity level for many fruits (such as apples, oranges, or pears) and root vegetables (such as potatoes, turnips, carrots, beets, and onions). Winter squash and pumpkins also do well in a root cellar.

CLOSET—A closet can be a very useful food pantry. A closet has all the recommended essentials: it's dark, temperature-controlled, and easily accessible. It's ideal to have a shelving or storage system that keeps food 6 inches off the floor to protect it in case of flooding.

UNDER THE BED—Storing food under the bed is a great way to take advantage of unused space. This area is dark and typically in a controlled climate, and if food is in a plastic container, it should be well protected. Keep in mind that food kept under the bed needs to be in a container that can't be tampered with by pets. In our home, we have a plastic underbed container filled with vacuum-sealed beans and rice.

GET ORGANIZED

These steps will help keep your pantry easy to use and maintain:

- Label each container or package with the contents, packing date, and any necessary instructions.
- Assign locations within the storage area to keep items organized (medical, baking, sanitation, breakfast, canned goods, and so on). Group items typically used together; for example, keep baking supplies (flour, sugar, baking soda, salt) next to each another for easy access.
- Place goods with the farthest-away expiration dates in the back and work forward to the nearest expiration dates.
- Systematically rotate and organize your storage. Check your storage inventory every six months to make sure items are properly rotated and used within their expiration dates.

3 PRESERVING YOUR FOOD

Preserving food is something of a lost art, in my opinion. What was once a necessary skill has now becoming a thing of the past. Coincidently, these skills were used in a time when refrigeration was not readily available and they would be great skills to learn in case we needed to live without the conveniences of electricity and our refrigerators for a given amount of time.

It is a fact that grid-down emergencies tend to last longer than expected. As the days of no electricity creep forward, you grow more concerned that your perishable food is going to begin spoiling. You realize it's time for action and want to take steps to preserve it. What if I told you that the typical contents of a refrigerator could all be canned or dehydrated to last up to twelve months longer? That's right, I'm talking about meats, vegetables and fruits, condiments, and juices.

In this chapter, I'm going to provide you with information on how to properly preserve these foods using techniques that were familiar to our ancestors. Throughout this book, when a recipe calls for a fresh ingredient or meat, you can replace it with dehydrated or canned goods that you've preserved on your own.

MAKING YOUR FOOD LAST

During the 1930s, my great-grandmother firmly believed in canning to make the most of the food they had. Canning was essentially her day's equivalent of the Tupperware that we have around today for leftovers. Back then, everything was canned to keep it for as long as possible. Nothing was wasted.

My Grandma Francis reminisces about her family's garden during the Depression: "Gardening was a family affair. The kids would pick the bugs off tomatoes and other vegetables so that Momma could put them up. She would put on her straw hat and get to working. When everything was picked, it was canning time. Momma could can anything, even fried chicken! She canned all of our leftovers so that they wouldn't go bad."

Preserving techniques can make most foods last on a pantry shelf for up to twelve months; preserved meats should be eaten within three to six months of processing. After a food's recommended shelf life has expired, natural chemical changes may affect its color, flavor, texture, or nutritional content.

Today those who preserve their own food may do so for economic reasons, as a way to embrace the past, or because they prefer knowing just where and how their food is grown. These are the principal methods of preserving food:

CANNING—By hermetically sealing food in a jar or can, the canning process destroys microorganisms and inactivates naturally occurring enzymes in food. Heating and then cooling the container forms a vacuum seal that keeps microorganisms from getting in. Acidic foods (such as tomatoes and certain fruits) can be processed or "canned" in boiling water—the "water bath method"—while low-acid vegetables and meats must be processed in a pressure canner at a higher temperature.

DEHYDRATING—Drying food is a very low-cost approach to use for long-term storage, and the dehydration process minimally affects the nutritional content. You can purchase a food dehydrator for as little as $40, or you can dehydrate foods in your oven at a very low setting. (Some people have even used their cars as a dehydrator during the hot summer months.) Dried foods will keep for six to twelve months.

FERMENTING AND PICKLING—This is a common way to preserve food, because the acidity level makes it difficult for bacteria to grow.

WHAT'S SO GREAT ABOUT PRESERVING FOODS?

Aside from providing you with a reliable food supply made to your own specifications, an added benefit of preserving food is that the vitamins and nutrients in most foods won't be destroyed during the process.

If you preserve berries, pears, apples, or apricots when they are almost ripe or at their peak, they are full of vitamins and antioxidants. A study at the University of Illinois Department of Food Science and Human Nutrition found that canned fruits and vegetables are nutritionally comparable to their fresh or frozen counterparts. The fermentation method of preserving food even adds vitamins.

FOOD SAFETY

Despite our best efforts, canned goods sometimes do go bad. Advises the National Center for Home Food Preservation, "Growth of spoilage bacteria and yeast produces gas, which pressurizes the food, swells lids, and breaks jar seals. As each stored jar is selected for use, examine its lid for tightness and a strong seal." In more cases than not, you will visibly notice or smell that spoilage has occurred.

Some clues that canned goods have spoiled:

- The jar or lid contains mold, and food has leaked out.
- The contents are discolored, cloudy, or slimy.
- The jar or can is swollen, and the contents may ooze out when you open it.
- The liquid in the jar looks as if it is bubbling.
- The contents have an "off" smell.

If you suspect that canned goods aren't safe, discard the jar and its contents.

BOTULISM

Clostridium botulinum—botulism—is a concern for anyone who cans their own food. Ingesting or even coming in contact with this contaminant can be fatal.

According to the Centers for Disease Control, on average there are 145 cases of botulism each year in the United States, of which approximately 15% are foodborne. Foodborne botulism most frequently comes from home-canned foods with low acid content (such as asparagus, green beans, beets, and corn), caused by failure to follow proper canning procedures.

The CDC advises that botulism can be destroyed by boiling home-canned food in the jar. Heating the canned food to an internal temperature of 185°F (85°C) for at least ten minutes will detoxify contaminated food or drink. However, it is best to err on the side of caution. If you suspect that food may be contaminated with botulism, discard the contents and can in its entirety.

Follow these safety tips when to avoid contact with botulism:

1. Wear rubber or heavy plastic gloves when handling suspect food or cleaning up contaminated surfaces and equipment.
2. Using a solution of 1 part unscented liquid household chlorine bleach (5% to 6% sodium hypochlorite) to 5 parts clean water, treat work surfaces and anything else that may have been contaminated, including can openers, utensils, and clothing. Spray or wet contaminated surfaces with the solution and let stand for 30 minutes.
3. Wearing gloves, wipe up the treated area with paper towels, being careful not to spread contamination. Seal the paper towels in a plastic bag before putting them in the trash.
4. Apply the bleach solution again, let stand for another 30 minutes, and rinse off with paper towels and discard in a plastic bag.
5. Discard your gloves when the cleaning process is complete. Thoroughly clean any contaminated clothing as well.

Truth be told, when I began reading about botulism and the serious health issues it causes, it made me not want to can food at all. Why take the risk? In the end, my desire to learn this skill and my need to provide healthy food for my family outweighed my fear. I educated myself and paid close attention to canning procedures and guidelines. I learned to trust my canning skills, and you can, too.

CANNING TECHNIQUES

If you have a way to boil water, you have a way to preserve food. There are two basic methods of canning: water bath canning and pressure canning. If you plan to preserve a great deal of food, you need to learn how to do both, since certain foods (low-acid vegetables and meats) require the higher temperatures of pressure canning to be safely canned.

WATER BATH CANNING

Jams and jellies, fruits, applesauce, pickles, and tomato products are all high-acid foods that can be safely preserved in a boiling water bath.

To prevent spoilage, the entire contents of your jar must be covered in liquid. You can preserve fruit in heavy, medium, or light sugar syrup, in a non-overpowering fruit juice such apple or white grape, or even in plain water.

MAKING SUGAR SYRUP

	2 cups sugar
+	4 cups water
=	5 cups light syrup

	3 cups sugar
+	4 cups water
=	5½ cups medium syrup

	4¾ cups sugar
+	4 cups water
=	6½ cups heavy syrup

Measure the sugar and water into a saucepan and cook over medium-high heat until the mixture comes to a boil. Then turn the heat down to low to keep the syrup warm. About 1 cup of syrup is needed for 1 quart of fruit.

Don't throw it out! Once you've used the contents of the jar, don't discard the syrup. Here are some ways to use it:

1. Sweeten beverages (powdered drink mixes, juices, teas).
2. Cook oatmeal.
3. Make fruit smoothies.
4. Make fruit drinks (mix 1 quart fruit syrup with 1 gallon water).
5. Thicken with cornstarch to drizzle on cake, pancakes, or waffles (mix 1 cup fruit syrup with 1 tablespoon cornstarch).
6. Marinate meats (acidic fruits in particular).
7. Replace the water in Jell-O recipes.
8. Sweeten a fruit salad.

9. Replace the liquid in cakes, cookies, or brownies.
10. Make a sweet rice dessert.

STEP-BY-STEP PROCESS

These are the basic tools you'll need in order to can properly and safely, using the water bath method:

- Jars
- Flats (snap lids)
- Rings

A large pot that is both wide and deep. The height of the pot needs to be at least 3 to 4 inches taller than the height of your canning jars.

- Rack (or a towel folded in the bottom of the pot)
- Jar lifter
- Jar funnel
- Labels

There are all sorts of other gadgets out there—such as magnetized lid lifters and tools for measuring headspace—but if you have the things on the this list, you are ready to can! So imagine a big pot of fruity jam bubbling away on the stove, ready to be canned. Doesn't it smell great?

1. Sanitize your jars, lids, and rings. You can wash them in a dishwasher, which will get hot enough to sterilize everything. Otherwise, you need to submerge them in boiling water for at least 10 minutes, lifting them carefully in and out with the jar lifter. Leave the sterilized items in the dishwasher or hot water until you're ready to use them.

2. Prepare your canner. Place your rack or folded towel in the bottom of the canner and fill the canner with water to the line on the inside. (If your canner doesn't have a line, fill to within 3 to 5 inches of the top.) Bring to a boil.

3. Fill your jars. Line up your jars on the counter near the stove. If the surface isn't heatproof, set them on a towel, because they'll be very hot when filled. Using the funnel, ladle in the prepared food, leaving the headspace recommended in your recipe.

4. Put on the lids. With a clean, dry dishtowel, carefully wipe the rims of the filled jars, making sure to remove any food residue. Place a flat on each jar, then twist on a ring—you don't have to really torque it.

5. Place the jars in the canner. Using your jar lifter, place the closed jars on the rack or towel in the canner. Be careful not to let them touch each other, because they could break if they bump together in the boiling water. Make sure the lids are completely submerged in the water.

6. Process the jars. Bring the water in the canner back to a

boil. Don't start clocking your processing time until the water is at a full boil. Then process the jars in the water bath for the amount of time specified in your recipe.

7. Remove the jars from the canner. Using your jar lifter, carefully remove the jars from the boiling water, one by one. Tip each jar to the side to allow the hot water to drip off the top, then place on your heatproof or towel-lined surface.

8. Allow 12 to 24 hours for the jars to cool and seal. Let the jars stand in a draft-free place where they won't be moved or bumped, usually for overnight. You'll hear a musical "pop" as a jar seals in the cool air—that's the lid being sucked down and forming a seal. When you are ready to store the jars, you can remove the rings and test the seals by pushing down with your finger. If a lid pops back and forth, it's not sealed; refrigerate to use right away. Store your sealed jars in a cool, dark place.

CANNING FRUIT: PROCESSING IN BOILING WATER BATH*

FRUIT	PREPARATION	COLD PACK METHOD	HOT PACK METHOD
Apples	Peel, core, and cut into halves, quarters, or smaller pieces.	Pack raw in hot, sterilized jars, cover with boiling-hot light sugar syrup (light). Process at once.	Boil in light syrup over medium-high heat until apples are heated through, about 6 minutes. Pack in sterilized jars. Process at once.
Applesauce	See page 147.	N/A	Pack in hot, sterilized jars and process.
Raspberries, Blackberries, Blueberries, Huckleberries	Pick over and rinse thoroughly; remove hulls.	Pack raw in sterilized jars. Cover with hot syrup (medium) and process.	Cover in juice or hot sugar syrup (medium), just enough to cover; cook until softened. Process at once.
Strawberries	Pick over and rinse thoroughly; remove stems.	N/A	For each quart of berries, add 1 cup sugar; let sit at room temperature until the juices flow. Boil rapidly for 5 minutes, then let sit overnight. Pack in sterilized jars in hot light to medium sugar syrup.

Note: Leave ½ inch headspace in each jar. Add 1 additional minute for each 1,000 feet of elevation above sea level for processing times of 20 minutes or less, 2 minutes for longer processing times.

*Chart inspired by The Settlement Cookbook, originally published in 1903.

FRUIT	PREPARATION	COLD PACK METHOD	HOT PACK METHOD
Cherries	Wash and remove pits and stems.	Pack raw in sterilized jars; cover with boiling syrup (thick syrup for sour cherries, medium for sweet cherries). Process immediately.	Mix syrup (medium for sweet cherries, thick for sour cherries) in a saucepan. Add cherries and cook over medium heat. Stir occasionally until sugar dissolves and mixture is heated. Pack in sterilized jars.
Peaches, Apricots, Nectarines	Drop peaches into boiling water to loosen the skins; peel. Cut fruit in halves or slices and remove the pits.	Rack raw in sterilized jars. Cover with hot sugar syrup (medium). Process immediately.	In a saucepan, add peaches and pour hot light to medium syrup over fruit until sugar has dissolved and mixture is heated. Pack hot peaches cavity-side down and pour syrup over. Process immediately.
Pineapple	Cut in thick slices, about 1/2 inch, then remove skin and core.	Pack raw in sterilized jars and cover with boiling light to medium sugar syrup. Process immediately.	Remove pits, add syrup, and boil over medium-low heat for 2 to 4 minutes, or until soft. Pack and process immediately.
Pears	Peel and remove the cores. Cut in halves or quarters; small pears can be left whole.	Pack raw in sterilized jars. Cover with sugar syrup (medium) and process immediately.	If pears are hard or whole, cook 4 to 8 minutes in boiling-hot syrup. For halved and quartered pears, over medium heat, warm pears in medium syrup for 5 minutes or until syrup is heated. Pack hot pears with their cavity down and process immediately.
Plums	Pit if desired by cutting plum in half (plums are usually processed with the skin on). If left whole, prick all over with a fork so syrup can penetrate.	Pack raw in hot jars. Cover with boiling sugar syrup (medium) and process immediately.	Bring sugar syrup to a boil and add the pitted plums. Bring to a rapid boil and then pack and process immediately.
Rhubarb	Cut in ½-inch pieces.	N/A	Place in a baking dish with ¼ the amount of sugar as rhubarb, by volume. Cover and bake at 350°F for 30 to 35 minutes, or until tender. Pack hot in sterilized jars and process immediately.
Tomatoes	Pour boiling water over to loosen the skins. Remove stems, cores, and skins. Leave whole, or halve or quarter.	Pack raw in sterilized jars and cover with boiling water. Add 1 teaspoon salt to each quart jar. Process immediately.	Over medium heat, add tomatoes to a saucepan and cover with water. Allow tomatoes to boil for 5 minutes and pack hot in sterilized jars. Add 1 teaspoon salt to each quart jar. Note: If canning whole tomatoes, do not layer them in saucepan.

FRUIT	COLD PACK	HOT PACK	PRESSURE COOKER
Apples	15 minutes	15 minutes	10 minutes at 5 pounds pressure
Applesauce	N/A	10 minutes	5 minutes at 5 pounds pressure
Raspberries, Blackberries, Blueberries, Huckleberries	20 minutes	15 minutes	10 minutes at 5 pounds pressure
Strawberries	N/A	15 minutes	5 minutes at 5 pounds pressure
Cherries	25 minutes	20 minutes	10 minutes at 5 pounds pressure
Peaches, Apricots, Nectarines	25 minutes	25 minutes	10 minutes at 5 pounds pressure
Pineapple	20 minutes	20 minutes	10 minutes at 5 pounds pressure
Pears	20 minutes	20 minutes	10 minutes at 5 pounds pressure
Plums	25 minutes	15 minutes	10 minutes at 5 pounds pressure
Rhubarb	N/A	10 minutes	5 minutes at 5 pounds pressure
Tomatoes	25 minutes	10 minutes	15 minutes at 5 pounds pressure

PECTIN OR NO PECTIN?

Pectin is a thickening and jelling agent commonly used in jams and jellies. It's available in powdered, liquid, and low-sugar varieties. You can also make your own (see the directions for Homemade Apple Pectin, on page 51). Pectin is naturally found in fruits and vegetables.

Depending on the type of fruit you are preserving, you may need to use more pectin or citric acid in your recipes. Pectin can be added by means of acidic fruit juices (such as apple, plum, or quince), or by using homemade or purchased pectin.

Since most fruits do not contain enough natural pectin to make preserves, it is helpful to know which fruits do. The following chart shows the naturally occurring pectin content of some popular fruits.

HIGH PECTIN CONTENT (Has enough natural pectin or acid for gel formation)	MEDIUM PECTIN CONTENT (May need additional pectin or acid)	LOW PECTIN CONTENT (Needs additional acid, pectin, or both)
Apples, tart (e.g., Granny Smith)	Apples, sweet	Apricots
Blackberries, sour	Blackberries	Blueberries
Crab apples	Cherries	Cherries, sweet
Cranberries	Chokeberries	Figs
Currants	Elderberries	Grapes
Gooseberries	Grapefruit juice	Guavas
Lemons	Grape juice	Nectarines
Loganberries	Loquats	Peaches
Plums	Oranges	Pears
Quinces		Plums
Raspberries		Pomegranates
Citrus skins		Strawberries

Homemade Apple Pectin

I think we can all agree that nothing compares to homemade. Making your own pectin for preserves is a rewarding all-natural way of using natural ingredients in your jams and jellies. *Makes 4 cups*

4 pounds tart, firm, ripe apples, peeled and cored

5 cups water

3 tablespoons lemon juice

1. Remove any bruised places on the fruit. Cut into thin slices and place in a large stockpot with the water and lemon juice. Bring to a boil, uncovered, for about 30 minutes or until the liquid reduces by half, stirring occasionally.

2. Line a strainer with a single layer of cheesecloth; set over a large pot. Pour in the apples and cooking liquid.

3. Gather the cheesecloth containing the apple pulp and squeeze it to extract any additional juice. Pour the strained juice into a measuring bowl.

4. Pour the juice back into the stockpot and boil for an additional 20 minutes. It should reduce to about 4 cups.

5. Remove from the heat and let stand for 10 minutes. Strain again, using another single

layer of cheesecloth to line your strainer.

6. Use the cooked juice stock as your homemade pectin. Four cups of this stock equals about a half-bottle (3 ounces) of commercial pectin.

7. Store leftover pectin in the refrigerator, or freeze for up to a year. You can also seal the pectin in sterilized pint jars while it is still hot and process it for 15 minutes in a boiling water bath.

No Pectin Apple Jelly

Don't throw those apples away! Use the apples from this recipe to make applesauce. *Makes 8 (½-pint) jars*

3 pounds apples, cored and quartered (peels left on)

3 cups water

3 cups sugar

1 tablespoon lemon juice (optional)

1. In a large uncovered pot, combine quartered apples and water over high heat and allow mixture to boil for 20 minutes until soft.

2. Strain the cooking liquid through a cheesecloth-lined strainer. Squeeze the cheesecloth to extract as much liquid as possible from the apples. (If you want clear jelly, don't squeeze the cheesecloth.)

3. Measure the strained liquid. For every 1 cup of juice, add 1 cup sugar. Boil together for 20 to 30 minutes. Stir frequently, ensuring that mixture is not sticking to the bottom. Allow mixture to come to the jelly point.

4. Pour mixture into hot, sterile jars, leaving ¼ inch headspace. Remove any air bubbles by inserting a knife and moving it around the jar in an up-and-down motion. Wipe rims of jars with a damp, clean paper towel. Adjust lids and rings and process in a water bath for 10 to 15 minutes.

TESTING FOR JELLY POINT

To test if jam or jelly is done, use a jelly or candy thermometer to make sure the mixture has come to 220°F. (If you live at a higher altitude, follow the recommended temperature for your area.)

If you don't have a jelly or candy thermometer, try one of these tests:

- Dip a cool metal spoon into the jelly. Turn the spoon on its side on a dish. If the mixture comes off the spoon in a large drop, it's done.

- Place a small saucer in the freezer while you're preparing the jelly. When you think the jelly is done, place 1 tablespoon hot jelly on the chilled saucer and return it to the freezer for 2 minutes. If you can divide the mixture in half with your finger, the jelly point has been reached.

No Pectin Peach Jelly

Makes 8 (½-pint) jars

5 pounds peaches, peeled, pitted, and coarsely chopped (11 to 12 cups)

4 cups sugar

4 to 6 tablespoons lemon juice

1. Combine the peaches and sugar in a large saucepan over medium-high heat. Slowly bring the mixture to a boil, stirring, until the sugar is completely dissolved.

2. Boil rapidly for 30 minutes, stirring frequently. Test to make sure the jelly point has been reached. Strain fruit pieces from liquid.

3. Ladle liquid into sterilized jars, leaving ½ inch headspace. Remove any air bubbles by inserting a knife and moving it around the jar in an up-and-down motion. Wipe the jar rims clean with a moistened paper towel, add the lids, and screw on the bands.

4. Process in a boiling water bath for 20 minutes.

Berry Jam

Makes 2 to 3 cups

5 cups berries (your choice)

1 (1.75-ounce) package no-sugar pectin

5 cups sugar

2 tablespoons lemon juice

1. In large a saucepan over high heat, mix together the berries and pectin and bring to a full boil. The berries will produce their own liquid when they cook down. Stir thoroughly to ensure the berries do not get scorched.

2. Stir in the sugar and lemon juice. Let come to a boil and test for jelly point. If jelly point has been reached, remove from the heat.

3. Fill sterilized jars with the jelly, leaving 1 inch of headspace. Remove any air bubbles by inserting a knife and moving it around the jar in an up-and-down motion. Wipe the jar rims clean with a moistened paper towel, add the lids, and screw on the bands.

4. Process in a boiling water bath for 10 minutes.

Ketchup

To easily peel the tomatoes for this recipe, submerge them in boiling water for 1 minute and then transfer to an ice-water bath. The skins will slide right off. *Makes 16 servings*

6 to 7 large tomatoes, quartered, seeds removed

1 small onion, chopped or ⅓ cup dehydrated chopped onions

3 garlic cloves, minced

1 bay leaf

6 tablespoons sugar

1 tablespoon dark molasses

¾ tablespoon garlic powder

¼ teaspoon ground allspice

1½ teaspoons paprika

¼ teaspoon ground cloves

2 teaspoons salt

¼ cup distilled white vinegar

1. Peel the skin from the tomatoes, cut them in half, and remove the seeds.

2. In a blender, puree tomatoes, onions and garlic.

3. Add to a large (12 to 16-quart) and bring mixture to an active simmer over medium-high heat.

4. Add the remaining ingredients and continue cooking, stirring frequently, until the sauce thickens.

5. Allow mixture to come to an active simmer and reduce heat to low for 20 minutes. Remove from the heat.

6. Fill sterilized jars with the ketchup, leaving 1 inch of headspace. Remove any air bubbles by inserting a knife and moving it around the jar in an up-and-down motion. Wipe the rims clean with a moistened paper towel, add the lids, and screw on the bands.

7. Process in a boiling water bath for 20 minutes.

BBQ Sauce

Serves 6

4 cups ketchup, purchased or made from recipe on page 54

1 jalapeño chile, left whole

2 cups water

1 cup apple cider vinegar

¼ cup packed light brown sugar

½ cup dark molasses

1 tablespoon freshly ground black pepper

1 tablespoon onion powder

1 tablespoon dry mustard

2 tablespoons lemon juice

2 tablespoons Worcestershire sauce

1. In a medium saucepan, combine all the ingredients. Bring to a boil over medium-high heat, reduce to simmer, and cook for 1 hour, uncovered, stirring frequently.

2. Remove jalapeño from mixture.

3. Fill sterilized jars with the sauce, leaving 1 inch of headspace. Remove any air bubbles by inserting a knife and moving it around the jar in an up-and-down motion. Wipe the rims clean with a moistened paper towel, add the lids, and screw on the bands.

4. Process in a boiling water bath for 20 minutes.

Enchilada Sauce

Makes 10 to 12 servings

3 tablespoons vegetable oil

3 tablespoons all-purpose flour

3 tablespoons chili powder

1 teaspoon ground cumin

½ teaspoon cayenne pepper, or to taste

3 cups water

2 (8-ounce) cans tomato paste

2 teaspoons garlic powder

1 teaspoon onion powder

1 cup prepared salsa (page 67)

salt and pepper

1. In a large pot over medium heat, whisk the oil, flour, and chili powder together and cook for 1 or 2 minutes.

2. Add the remaining ingredients and bring to a slow simmer. Stir well to combine the seasonings and dissolve the tomato paste in the water. Leave mixture uncovered and allow it to come to a slow simmer, for at least 20 minutes, stirring occasionally. Taste and adjust the seasoning as desired. The sauce will thicken as it cools.

3. Fill sterilized jars with the hot liquid, leaving 1 inch of headspace. Remove any air bubbles by inserting a knife and moving it around the jar in an up-and-down motion.

4. Wipe the rims clean with a moistened paper towel, add the lids, and screw on the bands.

5. Process in a boiling water bath for 20 minutes.

Teriyaki Sauce

Makes 15 servings

1 cup soy sauce

5 cups water

1½ tablespoons orange or pineapple juice

1½ tablespoons ground ginger

1½ teaspoons garlic powder

1½ cups packed light brown sugar

¼ cup honey

pepper, to taste

1 tablespoon sesame seeds

1. In a large bowl, stir together all the ingredients except for the sesame seeds.

2. In a large saucepan over low heat, toast the sesame seeds until toasted for 1 to 2 minutes. Pour in the mixture from the bowl and bring to an active simmer. Cook uncovered on low for 25 minutes, stirring often.

3. Fill sterilized jars with the hot liquid, leaving 2 inches of headspace. Remove any air bubbles by inserting a knife and moving it around the jar in an up-and-down motion. Wipe the rims clean with a moistened paper towel, add the lids, and screw on the bands.

4. Process in a boiling water bath for 20 minutes.

Meat variation. Sauté bite-sized boneless chicken pieces or beef pieces and add to the sauce before filling the sterilized jars; leave 2 inches headspace. Pressure-can for 90 minutes at 10 pounds pressure.

Sloppy Joe Sauce

Serves 4 to 6

1 tablespoon olive oil

½ medium green or red bell pepper, diced

½ cup chopped celery

1 medium onion, chopped or ¼ cup dehydrated chopped onion

4 garlic cloves, minced

½ cup shredded carrot

1 pound ground beef or 4 cups dehydrated ground beef crumbles

½ cup ketchup, purchased or from recipe on page 54

1 (6-ounce) can tomato paste

1 tablespoon Worcestershire sauce

1 tablespoon apple cider vinegar

2 tablespoons dark brown sugar

⅛ teaspoon ground cloves

½ teaspoon dried thyme

salt and pepper

1. Heat the olive oil in a large skillet over medium-high heat. Add the bell pepper, celery, and onion and sauté for 5 minutes. Add the minced garlic and shredded carrots; cook, stirring, for 5 more minutes. Remove from the heat and transfer the vegetables to a medium bowl; set aside.

2. In the same skillet over medium heat, cook the ground beef, breaking it apart with a spoon. Strain off all but 1 tablespoon of the fat from the meat.

3. Add the cooked vegetables to the skillet with the cooked ground beef. Stir in the wet ingredients and the brown sugar, mixing well. Add ground cloves, thyme, salt, and pepper. Lower the heat to medium-low and simmer for 10 minutes. Adjust the seasonings to taste, as needed.

4. Ladle into hot, sterilized quart jars, leaving 1 inch of headspace. Remove any air bubbles by inserting a knife and moving around the jar in an up-and-down motion. Wipe the rims clean with a moistened paper towel, add the lids, and screw on the bands.

8. Pressure-can the filled jars for 90 minutes at 10 pounds of pressure, following the manufacturer's directions for your pressure canner. Then turn off the heat and allow the pressure to return to zero naturally.

Plum Sauce

Makes 1 (10-serving) jar

1 cup plum jam

2 teaspoons grated orange zest

squeeze of lemon juice

1 tablespoon distilled white vinegar

1 teaspoon onion powder

¼ teaspoon ground ginger

¼ teaspoon ground allspice

dash of garlic salt

dash of red pepper flakes, optional

1. In a large saucepan, stir all the ingredients together to combine thoroughly. Bring to a boil over medium-low heat. Remove from heat.

2. Ladle hot sauce into a sterilized jar, leaving ¼ inch headspace. Remove any air bubbles and add the lid. Wipe rim and screw on band. Process in a boiling water bath for 20 minutes. Store for up to 1 year.

PRESSURE CANNING

Low-acid foods need to be preserved at a higher temperature than required for high-acid foods. A low-acid environment promotes the growth of bacteria (including botulism—see page 45), but the high temperatures achieved by pressure canning gets foods into the safety zone. The food must reach 240°F, which can only be achieved under pressure.

Vegetables (except for tomatoes, which are actually a fruit) are low in acid and must be processed in a pressure canner. Likewise, pressure canning must be used for meats, seafood, poultry, and soups.

VEGETABLE CANNING CHART FOR HOT PACK METHOD

VEGETABLE	PREPARATION	HOT PACK METHOD	PRESSURE COOKER PROCESSING FOR PINTS*	PRESSURE COOKER PROCESSING FOR QUARTS
Asparagus	Remove tough ends; cut to fit jars. Tie in bundles and cook in open saucepan for 2 minutes.	Place in sterilized jars and cover with hot water.	30 minutes at 10 pounds of pressure	40 minutes at 10 pounds of pressure
Beans, snap	Cut in small pieces. Add boiling water to barely cover. Boil for 5 minutes, uncovered.	Pack in hot, sterilized jars. Add 1 teaspoon salt to each quart jar. Cover with hot cooking liquid.	20 minutes at 10 pounds of pressure	25 minutes at 10 pounds of pressure
Beets	Use young beets. Remove tops and skins, leaving bottom roots. Boil for 20 to 25 minutes in water.	Pack hot in sterilized jars. Add 1 teaspoon salt to each quart. Cover with boiling water.	30 minutes at 10 pounds of pressure	35 minutes at 10 pounds of pressure
Carrots	Using only young carrots, cut off tops and peel.	Pack whole or sliced in hot, sterilized jars. Add 1 teaspoon salt to each quart jar. Cover with boiling water.	25 minutes at 10 pounds of pressure	30 minutes at 10 pounds of pressure
Corn	Use tender, young corn. Remove husk and silk; cut kernels from cob.	Fill jars with corn kernels to 1 inch from the top. Fill jars to 1 inch from top with boiling water.	55 minutes at 10 pounds of pressure	85 minutes at 10 pounds of pressure
Lima beans	Use young, tender beans. Shell.	In a pot, add enough water to cover and bring to a boil. Pack in sterilized jars and cover with hot liquid.	40 minutes at 10 pounds of pressure	50 minutes at 10 pounds of pressure
Okra	Remove stems, cover with water, and bring to a boil.	Pack in hot sterilized jars. Cover with hot cooking water.	25 minutes at 10 pounds of pressure	40 minutes at 10 pounds of pressure
Peas	Use only young, tender peas. Shell.	Place in a saucepan with boiling water and heat. Pack in sterilized jars and add 1 teaspoon salt to each quart jar. Process immediately.	40 minutes at 10 pounds of pressure	40 minutes at 10 pounds of pressure

VEGETABLE	PREPARATION	HOT PACK METHOD	PRESSURE COOKER PROCESSING FOR PINTS*	PRESSURE COOKER PROCESSING FOR QUARTS*
Peppers	Remove skins and seeds and cut into desired size.	Pack in hot jars, layering the peppers, with 1 teaspoon salt per pint. Water doesn't need to be added.	30 minutes at 10 pounds of pressure	40 minutes
Potatoes (white)	Peel potatoes and cut into 1" to 2" chunks.	Pack hot and cover with boiling water.	35 minutes at 10 pounds of pressure	40 minutes
Potatoes (sweet)	Boil 20 to 30 minutes until tender in center. Drain water and slip skins off and leave whole or cut into quarters or cubes.	Pack dry to top of can or to within 1" of jar top. Add ½ teaspoon salt to pints, and 1 teaspoon to quarts. Cover with fresh boiling water or hot sugar syrup (medium), leaving ¼" headspace.	65 minutes at 10 pounds of pressure	90 minutes
Pumpkin Winter Squash	Remove skin and seeds and cut into cubes.	Steam until tender. Pack hot to 1" from jar top in jar. Add 1 teaspoon salt per quart, or spices and brown sugar.	55 minutes at 10 pounds of pressure	90 minutes

*If processing in an altitude over 1,000 feet above sea level, process at 15 pounds of pressure.

Chart inspired by The Settlement Cookbook, published in 1903

STEP-BY-STEP PROCESS

For pressure canning, you'll need this basic equipment:

Jars

Flats (also called snap lids)

Rings

Pressure canner with valves, seals, and gauges

Rack (or use a folded towel in the bottom of the pot)

Jar lifter

Jar funnel

Just as for water bath canning, you can get lots of gadgets if you want to, but these are the essentials.

A number of the pressure canning steps are identical to those for water bath canning. The differences are related to the equipment. Once you've learned to use your pressure canner correctly, you'll find it every bit as easy as water bath canning.

1. Sanitize your jars, lids, and rings. You can wash them in a dishwasher, which will get hot enough to sterilize everything.

Otherwise, you need to submerge them in boiling water for at least 10 minutes, lifting them carefully in and out with the jar lifter. Leave the sterilized items in the dishwasher or hot water until you're ready to use them.

2. Prepare your canner. Place your rack or folded towel in the bottom of the canner and add about 3 inches of water. In pressure canning it's not necessary for the water to cover the lids. (Always check the instructions that came with your canner and follow those.) At this point, you can turn the burner on low to begin warming the water, but don't bring it to a boil yet.

3. Fill your jars. Line up your jars on the counter near the stove. If the surface isn't heatproof, set them on a towel, because they'll be very hot when filled. Using the funnel, ladle in the prepared food, leaving the headspace recommended in your recipe.

4. Put on the lids. With a clean, dry dishtowel, carefully wipe the rims of the filled jars, making sure to remove any food residue. Place a flat on each jar, then twist on a ring—you don't have to really torque it.

5. Place the jars in the canner. Place the closed jars on the rack or towel inside the canner. Be careful not to let them touch each other—not only could they break if they bump together in the boiling water, but in pressure canning the steam must be able to circulate all around the jars.

6. Build steam in the canner. Lightly apply cooking oil or Vaseline around the rim of the pressure canner lid so that it won't stick when you open it. Also check the vent pipe before each use to be sure it's clear. Place the lid firmly on the canner, latch it, and turn up the heat to bring the water to a boil. At this point, steam should be coming out of the vent pipe. Reduce the heat until a moderate amount of steam comes steadily out for 10 minutes. This is to release the air and build up the steam inside the canner.

7. Pressurize the canner. After exhausting the steam for 10 minutes, either close the petcock or place the weighted regulator on the vent pipe, depending on your canner. Turn up the heat and wait until the gauge has reached the desired pressure. (The required pressure will differ, depending on the altitude and the recipe.) This usually takes 3 to 5 minutes. (Note: if you lose pressure during processing, you must restart the processing time.)

Adjust the heat to maintain the pressure—this takes practice. Monitor your canner throughout the entire processing time to be sure the pressure is maintained.

8. Release the pressure. When your processing time is over, it's time to release the pressure. It couldn't be easier. Turn off the burner. Take the canner off the burner and set it on a heatproof surface. Walk away. Allow the canner to return to room temperature and release pressure naturally.

   The pressure is completely reduced when the air vent/cover lock and overpressure plug have dropped and no steam escapes when the pressure regulator is tilted. This can take 45 minutes to an hour and cannot be rushed!

9. Open the vent. When the pressure is completely gone, open the petcock or remove the weighted regulator. Leave the lid on for another 2 to 5 minutes.

10. Remove the jars from the canner. Very carefully remove the canner lid, facing it away from you so that you aren't burned by the steam rushing out. Using your jar lifter, carefully remove the jars from the canner, one by one. Tip each jar to the side to allow the hot water to drip off the top, then place on your heatproof or towel-lined surface.

11. Allow 12 to 24 hours for the jars to cool and seal. Let the jars stand in a draft-free place where they won't be moved or bumped, usually for overnight. You'll hear a musical "pop" as a jar seals in the cool air—that's the lid being sucked down and forming a seal. When you are ready to store the jars, you can remove the rings and test the seals by pushing down with your finger. If a lid pops back and forth, it's not sealed; refrigerate to use right away. Store your sealed jars in a cool, dark place.

CANNING JUICES

If you have a surplus of fruit in your home, canning juice is a great way to store it. Having canned juices in your emergency food pantry provides a low-cost alternative to store-bought juices, and they can be used for food preparation or canning as well.

An average of 15 pounds of whole fruit is needed per canner load of 7 quart-size jars. There are two ways to turn your fruit into juice:

- **JUICER METHOD**—If you have a juicer, you can be more efficient with your time. Simply follow the instructions for your juicer. Make sure that you read the section on pasteurizing juice in order to prolong the shelf life of your canned juice.

- **STOVETOP METHOD**—This may take more time, but with this method you'll be able to use the fruit for other recipes after the juice is extracted, thus making better use of your fruit. For example, for apple juice you can cook the apples on the stove, can the juice, and then use the apples to make applesauce. It's two canning projects in one!

PASTEURIZING JUICE

If you're canning juice, you may want to consider pasteurizing it. The Federal Drug Administration recommends that all juice be pasteurized. The pasteurization process heats juice in a high temperature environment for a short time to destroy bacteria, molds, and unwanted microorganisms that could be lurking in it. The drawback is that it kills off the good stuff, too. Most of the nutrients and minerals present in fresh juice are destroyed in the process. So why would you want to can nutrient-depleted juices? Well, having it on hand can provide you with more beverage options as well as ingredients for cooking.

HERE'S HOW TO PASTEURIZE JUICE:

1. Fill a sink with cold water.
2. Sterilize all utensils that will touch the juice. Jars, lids, funnel, and ladles should be placed in boiling water for 10 minutes.
3. Use a sterilized colander lined with a coffee filter to strain the juice; remove any fruit pieces.
4. Heat the juice in the top of a double boiler, maintaining a constant temperature of 175°F for 20 minutes.
5. Ladle the juice into the jars, leaving ½ inch headspace; secure the lids.
6. Place the jars in a sink of cold water and use a cooking thermometer to check that the water bath is at 40°F. Let the jars sit in the cold water bath for 15 minutes, continuing to monitor the temperature.
7. Remove the jars and store for up to 2 weeks in the refrigerator.
8. To can juice for longer-term storage, add the hot liquid to sterilized jars; add lids and wipe the rims. Screw bands on and process in a boiling water bath for 5 to 10 minutes.

Apple Juice

If you have an electric juicer, you can use it to extract concentrated juice, then add water to your liking. Home-canned apple juice has a shelf life of 18 months to 2 years. *Makes 6 servings*

8 to 10 sweet apples (such as Red Delicious, Gala, Fuji, or Rome, or use a combination)

10 cups water

½ to 1 cup granulated sugar (optional)

1. Core and slice the apples, but leave on the peels. Place in a large pot and pour in the water.

2. Cover the pot and bring the water to a boil over medium-high heat. Reduce to an active simmer and cook for 30 minutes, or until the apples are soft.

3. Discard any apple solids by straining the apple solids and separating them from the juice. If there are still solids present, use a coffee filter and strain again.

4. Sweeten the juice to taste.

5. Use the pasteurization process (page 63) to destroy any microorganisms.

6. Ladle the hot pasteurized juice into sterilized jars, leaving ¼ inch of headspace. Wipe the rims clean with a moistened paper towel, add the lids, and screw on the rings. In a hot water bath, process pint and quart jars for 5 minutes and half-gallon jars for 10 minutes.

Raspberry or Blackberry Juice

For drinking, dilute with 3 or 4 parts water to 1 part juice. *Serves 6*

3 to 4 pounds raspberries or blackberries

water

granulated sugar to taste

1. Place the berries in a large pot and add water to cover them. Bring to a boil over high heat, then remove from the burner and mash the berries to release the juices. Return the pot to the stove and bring the mixture back to a boil. Cook for 5 to 10 more minutes.

2. Remove from the heat and let cool for 5 to 10 minutes. Strain the cooled berry mixture through a colander lined with cheesecloth to remove any pulp or seeds. Mash any solid particles to extract any remaining juice. Sweeten to taste with sugar.

3. Use the pasteurization process (page 63) to destroy any microorganisms.

4. Ladle the hot pasteurized juice into sterilized jars, leaving ¼

CANNING OFF THE GRID

Familiarizing yourself with the two basic canning methods means that you'll have a better comfort level when attempting to preserve food when the grid is down—over an open fire in the back yard, for instance.

Consider how you might be able to bring a large pot of water to a boil without electricity. If you're lucky enough to have a woodstove with a flat surface in your home, you'll easily be able to can your harvest. But in the middle of summer—when produce is at its peak—a blazing fire inside your home is likely to be nearly unbearable.

Another option is an outdoor fireplace. You'll need a grill or cooking surface sturdy enough to hold a pot filled with water and at least half dozen jars of food. These are some possibilities:

- A brick or concrete fireplace with a fireproof cooking surface
- A firepit with a grill over the top
- A Mexican-style "beehive" oven

Make sure you have plenty of wood to burn to keep the heat high enough to maintain the pressure in a pressure canner or a hard boil in a water bath canner. You need to be able to tend the fire without moving your canning pot. You also need to have plenty of heavy towels and heat protection on hand for adding and removing jars. Use extreme caution when cooking over an open fire.

Stock up on basic supplies now so they'll be available in times of emergency—lids, rings, jars, pectin, vinegar, salt, and sugar.

Learning to can before there's an emergency will help you to adapt in the event the grid goes down. Personally, my first two attempts at jam-making resulted in...well, let's call it syrup, or perhaps ice cream topping. I was able to figure out how to improve my process and stock up on a type of pectin that works better for me. But if my first attempt had occurred during a long-term disaster, I'd have been stuck with the supplies I had on hand.

inch of headspace. Wipe the rims clean with a moistened paper towel, add the lids, and screw on the rings.

5. Process in a boiling water bath for 5 to 10 minutes.

Grape Juice

Makes 10 ounces

10 pounds sweet grapes

3 cups water

1 cup sugar (optional)

1. Place the grapes in a large pot and add enough water to cover them (about 3 cups). Bring to a boil over high heat, stirring often. When mixture comes to a boil, remove from heat.

2. Pour the grape mixture into a cheesecloth-lined colander or fine mesh sieve and set over a large bowl. Mash the grapes to extract the juices. Discard any skins, seeds, or pulp. Refrigerate for 24 to 48 hours.

3. Strain the chilled juice through a coffee filter to remove any remaining solid particles. Add sugar, if desired.

4. To can juice, heat the mixture in a large pot to boiling and ladle it into sterilized jars, leaving ¼ inch headspace. Wipe the rims clean with a moistened paper towel, add the lids, and screw on the bands.

5. Process in a boiling water bath for 15 minutes for pint- or quart-size jars. For half-gallon jars, process 20 minutes.

Vegetable Stock

Makes 5 servings

2 tablespoons olive oil

2 carrots, peeled and chopped

2 parsnips, peeled and chopped

2 onions, whole

2 celery stalks, chopped

1 (28-ounce) can diced tomatoes

3 garlic cloves, smashed

1 teaspoon black peppercorns

5 cups water

1. Heat the olive oil in a large (12 to 16-quart) stockpot over medium heat. Add the carrots, parsnips, onions, and celery. Cover the pot and cook, stirring occasionally, until the vegetables are soft.

2. Add the remaining ingredients and bring to a gentle simmer over medium-low heat. Cook gently for about 1 hour, or until the flavors are well incorporated.

3. Strain the stock through a cheesecloth-lined colander or fine-mesh strainer and discard the vegetable solids and peppercorns.

4. Ladle into hot, sterilized jars, leaving 1 inch of headspace. Wipe the rims clean with a moistened paper towel, add the lids, and screw on the bands.

5. Process in a pressure canner. Over medium-high heat, bring the pressure canner to a boil. Vent the steam for 10 minutes, then close the vent. When the canner reaches 10 pounds of pressure, process pint jars for 30 minutes and quart jars for 35 minutes. Allow pressure to return to zero naturally before removing jars.

Salsa

Serves 5

2 (28-ounce) cans diced tomatoes

7 green onions, chopped, green tops included

3 tomatoes, peeled and diced

6 tomatillos, peeled and diced

1 bunch cilantro, finely chopped

2 jalapeño chiles, finely diced

juice of 2 lemons

9 garlic cloves, minced

3 tablespoons ground cumin

2 tablespoons chili powder

½ cup distilled white vinegar

¼ to ½ teaspoon cayenne pepper

1. Mix all the ingredients together in a large bowl.

2. Ladle the salsa into sterilized jars. Wipe the rims clean with a moistened paper towel, add the lids, and screw on the bands.

3. Process in a boiling water bath for 45 minutes.

PACKING MEAT

Preserving meat is a great way to have a protein source available during an extended emergency. Meat can be canned in its own juices, in soups, or as canned meals. The U.S. Department of Agriculture strongly suggests that you use a pressure canner for canning meat. Beef, lamb, pork, veal, venison, poultry, and bear can all be canned.

Choose quality chilled meat and remove any large bones and as much fat as possible. Soak strong-flavored game meats for 1 hour in brine water (1 tablespoon salt per 1 quart water), then rinse.

There are two methods for packing meat in jars (always check gauge pressure for your altitude):

HOT PACK—Precook meat to the rare stage by roasting, stewing, or browning it in a small amount of fat. Add 1 teaspoon of salt per quart to the jar, if you wish. Fill hot jars with meat pieces and add boiling broth, meat drippings, water, or tomato juice (especially for wild game), leaving 1 inch of headspace. Remove air bubbles and adjust the headspace if needed.

Wipe the jar rims with a dampened paper towel, add the lids and rings, and process.

RAW PACK—Add 1 teaspoon of salt to each quart jar, if desired. Fill hot jars with raw meat pieces, leaving 1 inch of headspace. Do not add liquid. Wipe the jar rims with a dampened paper towel, add the lids and rings, and process. Always check gauge pressure for your altitude.

Canned Meat

Chopped or ground meat can be substituted for boneless meat pieces. Simply prepare it as you would for any other canned meat recipe. *Serves 5*

1 pound boneless meat (beef, poultry, lamb, venison, ham, etc.)

canning salt

1. Sterilize your jars, lids, and rings.
2. Remove any fat from the meat. Cut the meat into ½ to 1-inch pieces.
3. Fill the jars with the meat, leaving 1 inch of headspace.
4. Add ½ teaspoon canning salt to each pint or 1 teaspoon to each quart. Wipe the rims clean with a moistened paper towel, add the lids, and screw on the bands.
5. Following the manufacturer's instructions, pressure-can the filled jars for 90 minutes at 10 pounds of pressure. Then turn off the heat and allow the pressure to drop to zero naturally.

For canned beef tips: mix 1 or 2 tablespoons of cornstarch with some of the broth to make gravy. Serve beef tips and gravy on a bed of rice.

Soup: To make a delicious soup, add water, vegetables (whatever you have on hand), a can of tomatoes, and some seasonings to the canned meat.

Meat Stock

Serves 5

3 to 5 pounds bone-in meat, any kind

12 cups water

1 onion, whole

5 garlic cloves (optional)

2 celery stalks, whole

salt, as needed

5 black peppercorns, whole

2 bay leaves

2 carrots, peeled, whole

2 parsnips, peeled, whole (optional, to add an earthy flavor)

1. In a large (12 to 16-quart) stockpot over medium-high heat, brown the meat on all sides. Add the water and remaining ingredients. Bring to a boil and then reduce the heat to low and allow to slowly simmer for 2 to 3 hours.

2. Remove from the heat, allow to cool, and refrigerate overnight.

3. Remove the fat that has solidified at the top. Remove the vegetables and strain the stock through a cheesecloth-lined colander.

4. Remove the meat from the stock. Heat the stock over medium-high heat until it just begins to boil.

5. Fill sterilized jars with the stock, leaving 1 inch of headspace. Remove any air bubbles by inserting a knife and moving it around the jar in an up-and-down motion. Wipe the rims clean with a moistened paper towel, add the lids, and screw on the bands.

6. Following the manufacturer's directions, pressure-can the filled jars for 90 minutes at 10 pounds of pressure. After 90 minutes, turn off heat and allow the pressure to drop to zero naturally.

Serving ideas: Use this stock for beef tips and broth, vegetable beef soup, vegetable beef stew, roast beef sandwiches, or barbecue beef.

Pea Soup with Bacon

Serves 5 to 6

1 (14-ounce) package dry split peas

1 onion, diced

2 bacon slices, cooked and crumbled

1 potato, peeled and diced

2 carrots, peeled and diced

7 cups chicken broth

salt and pepper

1. In a large stockpot over medium heat, combine the peas, onion, bacon, potato, carrots, and broth. Add salt and pepper to taste. Cover, bring to boil, and simmer for 1½ hours, stirring occasionally.

2. Fill sterilized jars with the soup, leaving 1 inch of headspace. Remove any air bubbles by inserting a knife and moving it around the jar in an up-and-down motion. Wipe the rims clean with a moistened paper towel, add the lids, and screw on the bands.

3. Following the manufacturer's instructions, pressure-can the jars at 10 pounds of pressure. Process pint-size jars for 70 minutes and quart jars for 90 minutes. Then turn off the heat and allow the pressure to return to zero.

Spaghetti Meat Sauce

A vegetarian version of this sauce can be made by omitting the ground beef. Pressure-can the filled jars at 11 pounds of pressure for 20 minutes for pint-size jars and 25 minutes for quarts. Then turn off the heat and allow the pressure to drop to zero naturally. *Serves 4 to 5*

2 onions, chopped

4 tablespoons olive oil

8 to 10 garlic cloves, chopped

1 to 2 pounds ground beef

1 cup red wine

4 (28-ounce) cans diced tomatoes

2 carrots, peeled and finely shredded

3 celery stalks, chopped

2 bay leaves

1 tablespoon Italian seasoning

1 tablespoon dried basil

salt and pepper

1. In a large pot over medium heat, sauté the onions in the olive oil for 2 to 3 minutes. Add the garlic and sauté another 3 minutes.

2. Add the ground beef and cook thoroughly, breaking up the meat with a spoon. Pour in the wine. Add the rest of the ingredients and allow to simmer for 30 minutes, uncovered.

3. Fill sterilized jars with the hot sauce, leaving 1 inch of headspace. Remove any air bubbles by inserting a knife and moving it around the jar in an up-and-down motion. Wipe the rims clean with a moistened paper towel, add the lids, and screw on the bands.

4. Following the manufacturer's instructions, pressure-can the filled pint-size jars for 60 minutes at 10 pounds of pressure and 70 minutes for quart-size jars. After the processing time has passed, turn off the heat and allow the pressure to drop to zero naturally.

Canned Hot Dogs

Makes 2 (quart-size) jars

12 uncooked hot dogs left whole

Place the hot dogs in sterilized jars without adding water; they will produce their own liquid. Wipe the rims clean with a moistened paper towel, add the lids, and screw on the bands.

Pressure-can at 10 pounds of pressure for 90 minutes. Turn off the heat and allow the pressure to drop to zero naturally.

Canned Meat Loaf

For this recipe, use sterilized wide-mouth jars. This recipe can also be used for canning meatballs. *Makes 5 (quart-size) jars*

5 pounds ground beef

1 to 2 cups dry breadcrumbs or crumbled crackers

2 teaspoons garlic salt

1 teaspoon paprika

½ teaspoon pepper

¼ cup dehydrated onion

¼ cup dehydrated bell pepper

1½ teaspoons hamburger seasoning

¾ cup ketchup (purchased or made from recipe on page 54)

1. In a large bowl, thoroughly mix all the ingredients together. Pack the mixture into wide-mouth jars, leaving 1½ inches of headspace.

2. With your fist, push the meat down in the middle to make an indentation. This will reduce the risk of grease spilling out of the lids.

3. Process at 10 pounds of pressure for 90 minutes. Turn off the heat and allow the pressure to drop to zero naturally.

Beef Chili

Serves 6 to 8

1 to 2 cups dried pinto beans, soaked in water overnight

2 pounds ground meat or 4 cups dehydrated beef crumbles

1 (14.5-ounce) can diced or stewed tomatoes

1 cup dried bell peppers, diced

½ cup dehydrated yellow onion or 1 cup finely minced fresh onion or 1 tablespoon onion powder

1 to 2 teaspoons dried garlic or 3 garlic cloves, minced

3 tablespoons chili powder

1 tablespoon garlic powder

1 tablespoon dried jalapeño or 1 fresh jalapeño, chopped

¼ teaspoon cayenne pepper

salt and pepper

1. Rinse the soaked beans, then cover with water and simmer for 1 hour over medium-high heat, stirring often to prevent scorching.

2. Add the meat to the beans. (If you're using fresh ground beef, cook it first and then add to beans.) Stir in the other ingredients, mixing well. Cover and cook over medium heat for about 2 more hours. Remove the lid and cook on low for another 30 minutes to allow the chili to thicken slightly.

3. Fill sterilized jars with the hot chili, leaving 1 inch of headspace. Remove any air bubbles by inserting a knife and moving it around the jar in an up-and-down motion. Wipe the rims clean with a moistened paper towel, add the lids, and screw on the bands.

4. Following the manufacturer directions, pressure-can the filled jars for 90 minutes at 10 pounds of pressure. After 90 minutes, turn off the heat and allow the pressure to drop to zero.

Sugar-Baked Ham

These directions are "per jar." This is a great way to put away those end-less leftovers after Christmas or Easter dinner! *Makes 1 (8-ounce) jar*

1 teaspoon prepared grainy mustard

3 tablespoons brown sugar

1 teaspoon apple cider vinegar

4 (½-inch-thick) slices of ham

4 whole cloves

1. Make a paste of the mustard, brown sugar, and vinegar. Spread the mixture on one side of each ham slice.

2. Tightly roll up each slice with the mustard mixture inside and insert into the sterilized jar. Top each ham roll with a clove. Do not add any liquid.

3. Wipe the rim clean with a moistened paper towel, add the lid, and screw on the band.

4. Process the ham in a pressure cooker for 40 minutes at 10 pounds of pressure. After 40 minutes, turn off and allow the pressure to drop to zero.

DEHYDRATING FOOD

For centuries, dehydrating food has been used as a means of survival. Many consider this to be the safest and most affordable preservation method, and the best way to preserve the flavors of foods.

The dehydration process removes moisture from food so that bacteria, yeast, and mold can't grow. Dehydration only mini-mally affects nutritional content and prolongs the shelf life of your foods! In fact, due to the low heat setting during the drying cycle and the gentle air flow, 3% to 5% percent of the nutritional content of food is lost. However, you can retain much of the thiamin, ribo-flavin, niacin, and minerals found in dried vegetables if you use the soaking water you use to reconstitute them to then cook them.

Dehydrating vegetables and fruits for long-term storage is a great way to get needed nutrition into diets with minimal investment. You can also use a dehydrator to dry herbs, make jerky, make fruit or vegetable leather, make spices, dry noodles, and even make dough ornaments!

There are several different types of home dehydrators:

Stackable food dehydrators consist of removable trays that stack, one on top of the other. Some units house the mechanics in the bottom, others are on top of the stack.

Box-type food dehydration units are rigid and have removable shelves. The mechanical parts are either in the bottom or back of the box.

Fan dehydrators use a built-in fan to blow warm air across the food. This speeds up the drying process.

Convection food dehydrators have a heater at the bottom of the unit, so the heat rises through the food and dries it.

And let's not forget the ultimate dehydrator that harnesses the sun's power. Solar drying can be as simple as spreading a layer of fruit or vegetables in the sun, but it can also be done in a special container that catches and captures the sun's heat. The USDA recommends using high-acid fruits and vegetables, such as apricots, tomatoes, and grapes (to make raisins) for this method of dehydration. (Perishable, low-acid foods such as meat and poultry may not be dried by this method.)

Use fresh produce at the peak of ripeness for dehydrating. When overly ripe fruits and vegetables are dehydrated, the texture typically isn't as crisp.

Some vegetables need to be blanched before you dehydrate them. Use the following chart as a guideline:

VEGETABLE	BLANCHING METHOD	BLANCHING TIME	DEHYDRATING TIME
Asparagus, cut	Steam or water	4 to 5 minutes	8 to 10 hours
Beans, green (cut)	Steam or water	2 minutes	12 hours
Broccoli, small flowerets	Steam or water	3 to 3½ minutes	10 hours
Brussels sprouts, halved	Steam or water	4 to 6 minutes	12+ hours
Cabbage	Steam or water	2 minutes	8 to 10 hours
Carrots and parsnips, sliced	Steam or water	4 minutes	12+ hours
Cauliflower, small flowerets	Steam or water	4 minutes	12+ hours

VEGETABLE	BLANCHING METHOD	BLANCHING TIME	DEHYDRATING TIME
Celery, sliced	Steam or water	2 minutes	12+ hours
Corn, on cob (cut kernels after blanching)	Steam or water	2 minutes	12+ hours
Eggplant, sliced	Steam or water	3 minutes	12+ hours
Peas, shelled	Steam or water	3 minutes	12+ hours
Potatoes	Steam or water	7 minutes	12+ hours
Spinach and collard greens, trimmed	Steam or water	2 minutes	12+ hours
Summer squash, sliced	Steam or water	2 minutes	12+ hours
Winter squash, cut in chunks	Steam or water	2 minutes	12+ hours

STORING DRY FOODS

Dehydrated food doesn't take up a lot of space, so it's easy to store it in an organized fashion. No need to be concerned with refrigerating it or freezing it; as long as the dried food is kept in a cool, dark area with low moisture, it will last for up to twelve months.

In most cases, dehydrated food should be consumed within a year. Any time after this and the nutrients will begin to break down, Follow these guidelines:

- Dehydrated fruits and vegetables will last for up to a year if properly stored.
- Dried meats should be consumed within two months. If they haven't been eaten after one month, store them in the refrigerator to prolong their freshness.
- Dried herbs can last for years.
- Dried noodles are best if eaten within a year.

REHYDRATING FOOD

Rehydrating dried foods is relatively straightforward: introduce it to liquid and wait. Most foods can be rehydrated simply by soaking them in water at room temperature. However, there are some foods that require warm water or another liquid to be used, And for that matter, you can get creative about the type of liquid you use. For example, rehydrating dried food in a vegetable stock will add a richer flavor. Or, using fruit juices to rehydrate dried fruit will create a sweeter flavor. Covering the soaking foods with a lid or cover will help expedite the rehydration process.

To rehydrate dried food requiring hot liquid: pour boiling water or liquid over the dried food and cover it with a lid. Let it sit for twenty to thirty minutes to absorb the moisture. If you're adding salt, do so after the rehydration process is completed.

Once the food is rehydrated, it will not look the same or have the exact texture it had before being dried. Use the following chart to estimate the amounts of dried food and amount of time needed to rehydrate the goods.

REHYDRATING DRIED FOOD

PRODUCT	WATER (added to 1 cup dried food)	SOAKING TIME (minimum)
VEGETABLES**		
Asparagus	2¼ cups	90 minutes
Beans, lima	2½ cups	90 minutes
Beans, green and snap	2½ cups	60 minutes
Beets	2¾ cups	90 minutes
Carrots	2¼ cups	60 minutes
Cabbage	3 cups	60 minutes
Corn	2¼ cups	30 minutes
Okra	3 cups	30 minutes
Onions	2 cups	30 minutes
Peas	2½ cups	30 minutes

PRODUCT	WATER (added to 1 cup dried food)	SOAKING TIME (minimum)
Pumpkin	3 cups	60 minutes
Squash	1¾ cups	60 minutes
Spinach	1 cup	30 minutes
Sweet Potatoes	1½ cups	30 minutes
Turnip Greens and other greens	1 cup	45 minutes
FRUITS*		
Apples, sliced	1½ cups	60 minutes
Pears, sliced	1¾ cups	75 minutes
Peaches, sliced	2 cups	75 minutes
GRAINS**		
Rice—White, brown, or wild	1 cup	60 minutes
Pasta	1 cup	60 minutes
Meats**		
Poultry	1 cup	30 minutes
Ground Beef Crumbles, Deli Meat	1 cup	30 minutes
Beans	1 cup	60 to 120 minutes
Textured Vegetable Protein	1 cup	30 minutes

Source: University of Georgia
*Fruits—Use room temperature water
** Vegetables, grains, and meats—Use boiling water

Fruit Leather

If you have a lot of fruit on hand that isn't being eaten, you can quickly turn it into fruit roll-ups. Some of my family's favorite fruits are apples, pears, strawberries, raspberries, blueberries, apricots, peaches, and plums. *Makes 1 baking sheet full of fruit leather*

2 to 3 pounds fresh fruit

½ cup water

sugar or other sweetener, as needed

1 teaspoon lemon juice (optional)

dash of cinnamon, nutmeg, or other spices (optional)

vegetable or olive oil, for brushing pan

OVEN METHOD

1. For stone fruits, remove the pits and chop the fruit. For apples or pears, peel, core, and chop. For grapes, remove the stems and seeds. Taste to see how sweet the fruit is. If it's very sweet, you won't need to add any sugar.

2. Place the fruit in a large saucepan. Add ½ cup water for every 4 cups chopped fruit. Bring to a simmer, cover, and cook over low heat for 10 to 15 minutes, or until the fruit is soft.

3. Use a blender or food mill to purée the fruit to a very smooth consistency.

4. Return the fruit to the saucepan. Add sugar in small amounts until the fruit is as sweet as you want it. Continue to simmer and stir until the sugar is completely dissolved and the purée has thickened, 5 to 10 minutes (or more).

5. To brighten the flavor and prevent food discoloration during the drying process, stir in the lemon juice, if using. If you wish, add cinnamon, nutmeg, or other spices.

6. Line a rimmed baking sheet with sturdy plastic wrap (the microwave-safe kind). Brush on a small amount of vegetable or olive oil to keep the fruit from sticking. Pour in the purée to a thickness of ⅛ to ¼ inch.

7. Place the baking sheet in the oven; don't let the plastic wrap touch the oven sides or racks, and make sure it hasn't folded back onto the purée. (If that happens, the purée won't dry out.) Heat the oven to the lowest setting (usually around 170°F). Use the convection setting if you have one—it will speed up the process. Let dry for as long as it takes to form fruit leather that's smooth and no longer sticky. We usually keep ours in the oven overnight, 8 to 12 hours.

8. Roll up in the plastic wrap and cut into strips, or use cookie cutters to cut the fruit leather into fun shapes. Store in an airtight container in a cool, dark place.

FOOD DEHYDRATOR METHOD

1. Follow steps 1 through 5 for the oven method (above).

2. Line food dehydrator trays with microwave-safe plastic wrap. Pour in the fruit purée to a thickness of ⅛ to ¼ inch.

3. Set the dehydrator to 135°F and let the fruit dehydrate for 8 to 12 hours. The fruit leather is ready when it is smooth and no longer sticky, and easy to peel.

4. Roll up the fruit leather and cut into strips in its plastic wrap, or use a cookie cutter to cut it into shapes. Store in a cool, dry place.

DEHYDRATED MEAT

Dehydrating meat is a minimalistic way of extending the shelf life of your meats. Realistically, you don't need any additional seasonings or special cures to dehydrate meat. Simply place it on a tray and turn on the dehydrator. Taking the extra step of cooking ground meats before dehydrating them helps give them a "crumbled" look.

Although the USDA recommends that poultry be cooked until it has heated to an internal temperature of 165°F before it is dehydrated, many people dehydrate raw poultry just like they would dehydrate raw beef. If you feel more comfortable cooking the poultry before dehydrating it, follow this procedure:

Cut poultry into thin slices ¼ inch thick and place on dehydrator trays or, if you are using the oven method to dehydrate, place sliced poultry on a cookie sheet. Maintain a constant dehydrator temperature of 130°F to 140°F during drying or in the oven at the lowest setting. Meat is best if used within a month of dehydrating.

PREPARING THE MEAT

Partially freeze meat to make slicing easier. The thickness of the meat strips will make a difference in the safety of the methods recommended in this book. Slice meat into ¼-inch strips. For tougher jerky, slice the meat with the grain; for tender jerky, slice across the grain. Trim off any excess fat to prevent the meat from going rancid. Marinating the jerky gives the meat added flavor.

Ground Meat

I recommend using only lean or extra-lean ground meat, either beef or poultry. Meat with high fat content produces beads of oil as it dehydrates, and these have to be blotted off throughout the drying process. Look for meat that has less than 15% fat content, preferably in the 7% to 10% range. *Makes 4 cups dried meat crumbles*

1 pound lean ground meat (beef, turkey, or chicken)

¾ cup dry breadcrumbs

salt and pepper

1. In a bowl, combine the ground meat and breadcrumbs.

2. In a skillet over medium heat, cook the meat mixture thoroughly, breaking it up with a spoon; season with salt and pepper to taste. Drain off the excess grease and allow the meat to cool for a few minutes.

3. Transfer to dehydrating trays and set the dehydrator to 145°F. Dehydrate for 2 or more hours, until the meat is completely dried. Dried meat crumbles can be safely stored in an airtight container in a cool, dark, low-moisture environment for up to 1 month, or in an airtight container at room temperature for up to 1 month or in the refrigerator for up to 6 months to a year.

Ham

Use a lean cut, well cured ham that is trimmed of fat. Cut a fully-cooked smoked ham into ¼-inch cubes or very thin slices. Spread a single layer of the cubes or slices on each dehydrator tray. Dry at 145°F for about 4 hours, stirring occasionally. Reduce the temperature to 130°F and continue drying and occasionally stirring until the meat is hard and thoroughly dried, about 2 more hours. Store dried ham pieces in an airtight container in the refrigerator for up to 1 month. To rehydrate, combine 1 cup of dried ham and 1 cup of boiling water in a saucepan. Cover and cook on low heat for about 1 hour.

Basic Meat Jerky

Cut across the grain of the meat for crispy jerky, and with the grain for chewy jerky. *Makes 50 to 60 strips*

- 3 to 4 pounds uncooked meat (beef, pork, or poultry), trimmed of fat
- 5 ounces liquid smoke
- 5 ounces soy sauce
- 5 tablespoons Worcestershire sauce
- 1 tablespoon salt
- 1 tablespoon pepper
- 1 tablespoon garlic powder
- ½ tablespoon onion powder

1. Trim the fat and slice the meat into very thin strips.

2. Mix the remaining ingredients in a small bowl. Place a layer of strips in a large bowl or crock and sprinkle on part of the seasoning mixture. Continue to layer and season until all the meat has been used.

3. Weigh down the meat with a plate or other heavy object. Cover and let marinate, refrigerated, for at least 12 hours.

4. Drain the strips and carefully pat dry with paper towels. Arrange on a rack in a shallow baking dish and bake in a 250°F oven until dehydrated, about 4 hours. Once removed from oven, allow jerky to air-dry for 24 hours, or use a dehydrator on the highest setting until the meat is completely dried, up to 6 hours.

Teriyaki Jerky

Makes about 50 strips

- 2 pounds uncooked meat (beef, pork, or poultry) trimmed of fat and sliced in thin strips
- ½ cup Worcestershire sauce
- ⅔ cup soy sauce
- 1 tablespoon liquid smoke
- 2 tablespoons honey
- 1 tablespoon granulated sugar
- 2 teaspoons pepper
- 2 teaspoons onion powder
- 1 tablespoon ground ginger
- 1 teaspoon paprika

1. Place the meat in a large bowl or crock.

2. In another bowl, stir together the remaining ingredients. Pour the marinade over the meat, cover, and refrigerate for 24 hours.

3. Drain off and discard the marinade and carefully pat the meat dry with a paper towel. Place the meat strips on dehydrator trays. Dehydrate at 250°F until the meat is completely dried, up to 6 hours. Store in an airtight in a jar.

Black Pepper Jerky

Makes about 50 strips

2 pounds uncooked meat (beef, pork, or poultry), trimmed of fat and sliced into strips

1 cup Worcestershire sauce

¼ cup soy sauce

2 tablespoons salt

3 tablespoons finely ground black pepper

1 tablespoon garlic powder

1 tablespoon onion powder

1 teaspoon paprika

1. Place the meat in a large bowl or crock.

2. In another large bowl, stir together the remaining ingredients. Pour the marinade over the meat, cover, and refrigerate for 24 hours.

3. Drain off and discard the marinade and place the meat on dehydrator trays. Dehydrate at 250°F until the meat is completely dried, up to 6 hours. Store airtight in a jar.

Savory Turkey Jerky

Makes 50 strips

2 pounds boneless uncooked turkey breast meat, thinly sliced

½ teaspoon liquid smoke

2 tablespoons teriyaki sauce

1 tablespoon granulated sugar

2 teaspoons paprika

¼ teaspoon dried oregano

¼ teaspoon dried sage

¼ teaspoon black pepper

1 tablespoon onion salt

1 tablespoon garlic salt

1 tablespoon celery salt

1. Remove the bones and any fat and skin from the turkey meat. Slice the meat into thin strips.

2. Combine all the remaining ingredients in a large bowl. Add the meat strips to the marinade. Cover and refrigerate overnight.

3. Drain off and discard the marinade. Lay the meat strips on dehydrator trays.

4. Dehydrate at the highest setting until the meat has dried out completely, up to 6 hours.

Dehydrated Seafood

Dehydrating seafood doesn't create the most pleasant odor. To avoid smelling up the house, plug in your dehydrator outdoors. Do this during the day so that you won't attract unwanted nighttime animal visitors.

Makes 3 ounces

1 pound medium or large shrimp

1 pound fish, deboned and filleted

1. To dehydrate fish or shellfish, remove any shells, devein shrimp, and remove any bones from fish.

2. Cut or break into small pieces.

3. In a large pot of boiling salted water, cook fish or shrimp 2 to 3 minutes until firm. Drain waste and pat meat dry with a paper towel.

4. Spread flat on a dehydrating tray. Dehydrate at 155°F for 4 to 6 hours, until crispy. Dried shrimp is best stored in an airtight container for up to 1 month at room temperature. Refrigerate to store longer.

Dried Soup Mixes

Premade dry soup mixes are a great emergency food to have stored away. All you need to do is add water, and you have an instant meal. Store the following soup mixes in airtight containers and plan to enjoy them within a year.

For the following recipes, 1 cup of dry mix yields 8 cups of soup. To serve, bring 8 cups of water to a boil in a 4-quart saucepan and add 1 cup of dry soup mix. Turn off the heat and cover the pan. Let it sit for 20 minutes, or until the soup mixture is tender.

The best way to dry vegetables for soup mixes is to whirl them in a blender until they're the size of small, minced flakes. Then spread on a dehydrating tray and dehydrate for 4 to 5 hours at 145°F, or until completely dry. Once dried, store in labeled wide-mouth pint-size jars.

VEGETABLE SOUP MIX

1 cup dried vegetable flakes (any combination: onions, peas, carrots, zucchini, squash, celery)

½ cup dried tomato purée

3 tablespoons onion flakes

½ cup pearl barley or lentils

1 teaspoon dried parsley

½ teaspoon garlic powder

½ teaspoon onion powder

3 tablespoons chicken or beef bouillon

salt and pepper

CREAMY COUNTRY SOUP MIX

2 cups nonfat dry milk

¼ cup chicken bouillon granules

3 tablespoons dried vegetable flakes (such as potatoes, corn, beans, carrots, zucchini, or squash)

2½ teaspoons onion powder

1 teaspoon dried chives

½ teaspoon dried thyme

¼ teaspoon garlic salt

2 teaspoons pepper

CREAMY POTATO SOUP MIX

2 cups instant potato flakes

2 tablespoons powdered butter

2 cups nonfat dry milk

2 tablespoons chicken bouillon granules

2 teaspoons dehydrated minced green onion

1 teaspoon dried parsley

½ teaspoon dried thyme

1¼ teaspoons seasoning salt

pepper, to taste

bacon bits or dried ham bits (optional)

CHICKEN AND RICE SOUP MIX

½ cup dried chicken pieces, stored separately from soup mix

1 cup dehydrated cooked white or brown rice (see page 139)

3 tablespoons chicken bouillon granules

2 tablespoons dried celery

2 tablespoons dried onion flakes

¼ cup dried carrots

2 teaspoons dried garlic flakes

½ teaspoon dried thyme

1 teaspoon white pepper

salt and black pepper, to taste

Rehydrate the chicken in water for 30 minutes before preparing soup. Then bring 8 cups of water (including the water from rehydrating the chicken) to a boil in a 4-quart saucepan over medium-high heat, and add 1 cup soup mix. Turn off the heat, cover, and let sit 20 minutes. Then turn the heat to low and simmer, covered, for 30 to 35 minutes, or until the rice is tender.

TURKEY NOODLE SOUP MIX

½ cup dried turkey bits

1 cup uncooked egg noodles

3 tablespoons chicken bouillon granules

1 tablespoon dried onion

1 tablespoon dried celery

½ tablespoon dried carrots

½ teaspoon dried thyme

⅛ teaspoon celery salt

½ teaspoon garlic powder

½ teaspoon pepper

1 bay leaf

For 8 servings, rehydrate the turkey in water for 30 minutes. Then bring a total of 8 cups of water (include the water for rehydrating the turkey) to a boil in a 4-quart saucepan over medium-high heat and add 1 cup of the soup mix. Turn the heat to low and simmer, covered, for 30 to 35 minutes, or until noodles and turkey are tender.

HEARTY BEAN SOUP MIX

- 2 cups dehydrated split peas
- 2 cups dehydrated small lima beans
- 2 cups dehydrated pinto beans
- 2 cups dehydrated Great Northern beans
- 1 cup dehydrated ham bits
- 1 cup dehydrated minced onions
- 1 cup dehydrated carrots
- 1 cup dehydrated celery
- ¼ cup dehydrated tomato purée
- 1½ teaspoons ground cumin
- 1 teaspoon dried marjoram
- 1½ teaspoons garlic powder
- 2 tablespoons chicken bouillon granules
- 1 teaspoon onion salt
- ¼ teaspoon pepper

To rehydrate beans, soak in cool water for 45 to 60 minutes, or cook in simmering water for 10 to 15 minutes. Rehydrate the ham in water for 30 minutes.

Bring 8 cups water (include the water for rehydrating the ham) to a boil in a 4-quart saucepan over medium-high heat, add rehydrated beans and 1 cup soup mix, and cook on medium-high heat for 30 minutes. Turn off the heat, cover, and let sit 20 minutes.

CREAMY CHEESE SOUP

- ¼ cup dehydrated sharp Cheddar cheese or 1 packet of powdered cheese mix from a box of macaroni and cheese
- 1 tablespoon chicken bouillon granules
- ½ teaspoon pepper
- ¼ cup dehydrated carrots
- 1 tablespoon onion powder
- 3 tablespoons celery salt
- 3 tablespoons dried parsley
- 3 cups dry nonfat milk or powdered coffee creamer
- 2 to 3 tablespoons instant mashed potatoes

Instant White Rice

Serves 4

- 1 cup uncooked white rice
- salt and pepper

Cook the rice according to the package directions, or follow the directions on page 139. Allow to cool and then spread evenly on a dehydrator tray. Dehydrate at 135°F for 12 hours. Halfway through the drying process, break up any rice that is stuck together. Store in an airtight container in a cool, dark place for up to 6 to 12 months.

Instant Brown Rice

Serves 4

2 cups brown rice

salt and pepper

Cook the rice according to the package directions, or follow the directions on page 139. Allow to cool. To dehydrate, cover your dehydrator trays with parchment paper or the mesh liners that came with your unit. Do not use waxed paper in your dehydrator as it will melt. Spread the rice in a single layer and dehydrate at 125°F for 5 hours or until completely dry. Halfway through the drying process, break up any rice that is stuck together. Allow to cool to room temperature before storing in an airtight container.

Dehydrated Beans

Dehydrating beans will expedite cooking times during extended emergencies and cut down on fuel usage.

1 pound small beans (such as pinto beans, navy beans, or lentils), uncooked

1. Rinse the beans in a colander under cool water to remove any grit.

2. Bring a large pot of water to a boil, add the beans, and cook until soft, 2 to 3 hours. Drain the beans in a colander to remove any excess water.

3. Lay the beans on the dehydrator tray in a single layer. Pat with towels to remove excess moisture. Arrange the beans so that air can circulate around them.

4. Set the temperature on the dehydrator to 140°F.

5. Place the tray in the dehydrator. Dry for 5 to 8 hours, turning the beans and rotating the trays every 2 to 3 hours to ensure even drying. Check the dryness periodically. When you touch the beans they should be dry and brittle and have no pockets of moisture present. Remove the tray from the dehydrator. Allow the beans to cool completely.

6. Place the beans in an airtight container such as a jar or plastic freezer bag. Store the beans in a cool, dark place.

7. To rehydrate, add 1 cup of boiling water to ¾ cup dehydrated beans and allow to sit for 15 to 20 minutes.

FERMENTING FOOD

Fermented foods are a staple in many cultures around the world. Before the days of electricity and canning, this was how food was stored for the long term. It's one of the simplest methods of home preservation, and only one that actually adds nutrition to food. Fermented food is "live" food, loaded with probiotics and healthy enzymes. Vitamins B and C are produced in abundance during the fermentation process.

Most vegetables can be fermented. Especially popular are cabbage (think sauerkraut or kimchee), beets, and mixtures of garden vegetables such as carrots and cauliflower. Here's how to do it:

1. Cut raw vegetables into bite-size pieces and place in a jar. Bruise them with a potato masher or pestle to release the juices.

2. Make a brine in the ratio of 1½ tablespoons salt to 1 cup filtered water. The water must be filtered and free of chlorine—do not use water straight from the tap.

3. Flavor your brine with whatever herbs and spices you like—such as dill, whole peppercorns, caraway seeds, basil, tarragon, bay leaves, or dried chiles. Alternatively, you can add the herbs and spices directly to the individual jars.

4. Pour the brine into the jar, leaving 1 to 2 inches of headspace; the mixture will bubble up inside the jar during the fermentation process. Seal tightly, using plastic lids, if possible; metal lids can be corroded by the salt in the brine.

5. Place on a baking sheet or tray to catch any drips and keep at room temperature for 5 to 10 days. Remove the lid to taste-test whether the veggies are soured to your liking, then reseal and move to a cool, dark place for 8 to 12 months.

Dried Breadcrumbs

Makes 1 cup

5 thin slices bread

Lay thinly sliced bread slices on a dehydrator tray and heat at 145°F for 2 to 3 hours, or until the bread easily crumbles. Crush into crumbs and store in an airtight plastic bag or jar away from moisture.

Dehydrated Noodles

Makes 8 servings

1 (16-ounce) bag dry egg noodles, cooked

Cook noodles according to directions, but undercook them by 2 to 3 minutes. Drain and allow to cool. Spread evenly on a dehydrator tray, ensuring that pasta is not touching and dehydrate and dry at 130°F for 2 to 4 hours or until the noodles are firm and completely dry. Once the pasta is completely dry (it should be brittle and crisp), it can be stored in an airtight container in a cool, dark space for up to 6 months. To rehydrate, add 1 cup boiling water to 1 cup dried pasta and allow to sit for 5 to 10 minutes, or until soft.

4 BREAKFAST

There's something to be said for breakfast being the most important meal of the day. You have to admit that after a good breakfast you have more energy, enhanced concentration, and a better overall mood. Experts suggest that a balanced breakfast kick-starts your metabolism and supplies a continuing source of energy throughout the day—and when an emergency occurs, you'll want to have that energy to keep up with whatever activity the situation calls for.

Breakfast can be an easy way to get needed protein, carbohydrates, and vitamins into your body. In a time of emergency, keep simplicity in mind—after all, your fuel may be limited or your food reserves may run low. A simple breakfast could be oatmeal, grits, toast with peanut butter, or dry cereal. That said, you may prefer a more substantial breakfast or just a change from the ordinary. The following recipes— using ingredients commonly stored in emergency food pantries—could easily be incorporated into your daily breakfast planning.

Griddle Cakes

Offer powdered sugar, fruit compote, or syrup to top these pancakes.

Makes 12

1½ cups fine unseasoned dry breadcrumbs

1½ cups hot milk

2 tablespoons butter, melted

2 eggs, well beaten

½ cup all-purpose flour

3½ teaspoons baking powder

½ teaspoon salt

1 tablespoon granulated sugar

1. Stir all the ingredients together in a large bowl to make the griddle cake batter.

2. Heat a greased skillet over medium heat.

3. Spoon batter into the skillet, using about ¼ cup for each griddle cake. Cook for 1 to 2 minutes on each side, or until golden brown. Serve warm.

Protein Pancakes

Serves 2

1 (1-ounce) scoop vanilla protein powder

water, as needed

1 tablespoon vegetable oil, vegetable shortening, or butter

pancake toppings (such as fruit, applesauce, or syrup)

1. Mix the protein powder with enough water to make a lumpy batter the same consistency as regular pancake batter.

2. Add oil, shortening, or butter to a hot skillet over medium heat until a drop of water dropped onto its surface sizzles.

3. Pour in batter by large spoonfuls and cook for 1 to 2 minutes on each side. Add your toppings of choice to serve.

Cinnamon Rolls

Makes 12 rolls

¾ cup milk

1 packet (2¼ teaspoons) active dry yeast

2 cups all-purpose flour

1 egg yolk

3 tablespoons powdered sugar

2½ tablespoons butter, melted

dash of salt

FILLING

3 tablespoons brown sugar

1 tablespoon ground cinnamon

¼ cup (½ stick) butter, softened

½ cup raisins (optional)

1. Heat the milk to lukewarm. In a small bowl, dissolve the yeast in the warm milk; whisk for 1 minute and set aside.

2. In a large bowl, combine the flour, egg yolk, powdered sugar, melted butter, and salt. Mix for 8 minutes or until the dough becomes smooth and no longer sticks to a wooden spoon.

3. Cover the dough with greased plastic wrap and place in the refrigerator for 3 to 24 hours. Bring to room temperature before shaping.

4. In a small bowl, combine all the ingredients for the filling and mix well. Set aside.

5. On a floured surface, roll the dough into a 12 x 9-inch rectangle. Spread the dough with the filling mixture. Sprinkle with raisins, if desired.

6. Roll the dough from the long side, jelly-roll style; pinch the seam to seal. Cut into 12 equal-size pieces and place in lightly greased muffin cups. Cover and let rise in a warm place until doubled in size, about 30 minutes. Preheat the oven to 375°F.

7. Bake for 20 minutes, or until lightly browned. Remove from the muffin tin and let cool on a wire rack. Serve warm.

Homemade Cake Donuts

Makes 16

1 cup granulated sugar

4 teaspoons baking powder

1½ teaspoons salt

½ teaspoon ground allspice

2 eggs, lightly beaten

1 cup milk

¼ cup (½ stick) butter, melted

3 cups all-purpose flour

vegetable oil for frying

COATING

2 to 3 tablespoons granulated or powdered sugar

⅛ teaspoon ground cinnamon

1. In a large bowl, stir together the sugar, baking powder, salt, and allspice.

2. Stir in the eggs, milk, and melted butter. Add the flour 1 cup at a time, beating until blended. The dough should be soft and sticky but firm enough to handle. Cover with plastic wrap and chill for 1 hour.

3. Remove the chilled dough from the refrigerator. Begin heating about 1 inch of oil to 360°F in a large skillet.

4. Working on a floured surface with half the dough at a time, roll to about ½ inch thickness.

Cut circles using the floured top of a glass. Use your thumb to make a hole in the center of each circle.

5. Gently drop the doughnuts in batches into the hot oil. Flip them over as they puff; turn a couple more times as they cook, about 2 to 3 minutes total or

until golden. Remove from the oil and place on paper towels to drain.

6. Mix the sugar and cinnamon in a paper bag. Carefully shake the warm donuts in the bag, one at a time, to cover with the sugar mixture.

Applesauce Oat Muffins

Makes 12

2 (1-ounce) packets instant plain oatmeal

1¼ cups all-purpose flour

½ cup sugar

½ teaspoon baking soda

1 teaspoon baking powder

¼ teaspoon salt

1 teaspoon apple pie seasoning (page 21)

1 cup buttermilk

1 egg

⅔ cup applesauce

½ teaspoon vanilla extract

1. Preheat the oven to 400°F. Grease the cups of a standard 12-cup muffin tin.

2. Mix all the dry ingredients together in a medium bowl (oatmeal through apple pie seasoning).

3. In a large bowl, whisk together the buttermilk, egg, applesauce, and vanilla. Combine with the dry ingredients, mixing just until well incorporated.

4. Spoon into the prepared muffin tin. Bake for 12 minutes, or until golden brown on top.

Egg in the Middle

Serves 4

4 slices bread

3 eggs

4 tablespoons butter

salt and pepper

1. On a cutting board, use a cookie cutter or small round cup to cut a 3-inch hole in the middle of

each slice of bread. Keep the holes and toast them while the eggs are being prepared.

2. In a small bowl, whisk the eggs until well mixed.

3. In a skillet over medium heat, melt 1 tablespoon of the butter. Add a slice of bread, flipping it

so that both sides are coated in butter.

4. When the bread begins to toast on one side, ladle about ¼ of the beaten eggs into the hole in the bread. When the egg mixture begins to cook and adhere to the bread, turn the bread over to cook the other side.

5. Sprinkle with salt and pepper and serve immediately. Repeat for each slice of bread.

Luke's Sliced Grits

Serves 4

3 cups water

1 teaspoon salt

1 cup plain grits or yellow cornmeal

1 teaspoon granulated sugar

2 to 3 tablespoons unsalted butter

maple syrup, powdered sugar, or pecans, for serving

1. In a medium saucepan, heat the water to boiling on high. Reduce the heat to medium; stir in the salt and cornmeal.

2. Reduce the heat to low and add the sugar. Cook, stirring regularly, until the mixture is thick, about 10 minutes.

3. Spoon into a lightly greased 9 x 5-inch loaf pan. Cover and refrigerate overnight.

4. In the morning, melt the butter in a skillet over medium heat. Cut the cornmeal mush into 1-inch-thick slices. When the butter is melted, add slices of grits. Cook on one side for 5 minutes, turn, and cook 5 minutes more (add more butter or oil before cooking the second side, if desired).

5. To serve, drizzle with maple syrup, sprinkle with powdered sugar, or top with pecans.

Southern Biscuits and Gravy

Southern cooks are real pros at taking a small amount of something and making it feed a lot of people. Biscuits and gravy is one of those creations—how else can you make half a pound of bacon, ham, or sausage feed four hungry people and leave them thoroughly satisfied? *Serves 4*

BISCUITS

2 cups all-purpose flour

1 tablespoon baking powder

½ teaspoon salt

½ cup vegetable shortening

¾ cup milk

1. Preheat the oven to 450°F.

2. In a large mixing bowl, sift together the flour, baking powder, and salt. Cut in the shortening with a fork or pastry blender until the mixture resembles coarse crumbs. Pour

in the milk while stirring with a fork. Mix until the dough is soft and moist and pulls away from the sides of the bowl.

3. Turn out the dough onto a lightly floured surface and toss with flour until no longer sticky. Roll to ½ inch thickness.

4. Cut out your biscuits using a floured biscuit cutter, cookie cutter, or glass top. Press together the dough scraps and cut more biscuits.

5. Place the biscuits on an ungreased baking sheet. Bake until golden brown, about 10 minutes.

BREAKFAST GRAVY

Breakfast gravy, by its very nature, is not healthy, low in cholesterol, or heart-friendly. It is, however, a tasty source of calories and protein that can power you through a morning of hard physical labor.

½ pound bacon, sausage, or ½ cup ham, or ¼ cup dehydrated meat crumbles

3 tablespoons vegetable shortening or butter

¼ cup all-purpose flour

3 cups milk (can be reconstituted nonfat dry milk)

salt and pepper to taste

1. In a large cast-iron skillet, brown the meat, breaking it into bite-size pieces. If using ham, cut into cubes before browning.

2. Add the shortening and flour to the pan, stirring constantly to create a roux.

3. When the roux begins to brown lightly, stir in the milk; season with salt and pepper. Stir constantly until your gravy is the consistency you want.

4. Serve over fresh-baked biscuits.

Easy French Toast

Serves 4

1 egg

1 cup milk

1 tablespoon ground cinnamon

1 teaspoon vanilla extract

¼ teaspoon finely grated orange zest

dash of salt

4 slices bread

butter or oil, as needed

syrup or jam, for serving

1. In a large bowl, whisk together the egg, milk, cinnamon, vanilla, orange zest, and salt.

2. Over medium heat, melt butter or oil in a skillet until a drop of water dropped onto the surface sizzles.

3. Dip the bread slices in the egg mixture to coat thoroughly.

4. Cook, turning once, until both sides of the bread are lightly browned and crisp. Serve hot, topped with syrup or jam.

Breakfast Quinoa

Serves 6

1 cup milk

1 cup water

1 cup quinoa

½ teaspoon ground cinnamon

¼ teaspoon ground cumin

fresh or dehydrated fruit, such as strawberries, blackberries or apples (optional)

⅓ cup chopped toasted pecans

6 teaspoons honey

1. Combine the milk, water, and quinoa in a medium saucepan and bring to a boil over medium heat.

2. Reduce the heat to low; cover and simmer 15 minutes, or until most of the liquid has been absorbed. Turn off the heat; let stand on the burner, covered, for 5 minutes.

3. Stir in the cinnamon, cumin, and fruit, if using. Top each serving with pecans and drizzle with 1 teaspoon honey.

Creamy Grits

Serves 6

4 cups water, or more as needed

¼ teaspoon salt

1 cup grits (not instant)

¼ teaspoon ground cinnamon

cream or milk, for serving

toasted almonds, dried fruit, honey, maple or fruit syrup (optional)

1. In a medium saucepan over medium-high heat, bring the water to a boil. Stir in the salt and grits and reduce the heat to medium-low.

2. Cover saucepan with lid and allow the grits to simmer for at least 30 to 35 minutes, until soft.

3. If the grits become too thick or dry, add more water, ¼ cup at a time until the mixture is the right creamy consistency.

4. Spoon the warm grits in bowls with a splash of cream or milk and your choice of toppings.

Power Oatmeal

Serves 2

1 cup rolled oats

½ to 1 cup milk

1 (1-ounce) scoop vanilla protein powder

1 cup dried fruit (such as apples, berries, or raisins)

2 tablespoons chopped nuts (walnuts or pecans are delicious)

1. Cook the oats according to the package directions.

2. Add the milk and protein powder. Thoroughly stir the mixture until all ingredients are combined. Thoroughly mix in the protein powder.

3. Top the individual servings with fruit and nuts.

Instant Oatmeal Mix

Makes 14 half-cup servings

6 cups quick-cooking oats

⅓ cup dry powdered milk

¼ cup powdered sugar

¼ cup packed brown sugar

3 teaspoons ground cinnamon

1 teaspoon salt

1 cup dried fruit or nuts

1. In a large bowl, combine all of the ingredients. Then store in airtight container in a cool, dry place for up to 1 month.

2. To prepare oatmeal, place ½ cup of mix and add ½ cup boiling water or milk to the mix and stir until oats are softened, 2 to 3 minutes.

Homemade Bran Flakes

Serves 4

1 cup wheat bran

1 cup whole wheat flour

⅔ cup almond flour or other finely ground nuts

¼ cup packed light brown sugar

½ teaspoon baking powder

½ teaspoon salt

½ cup milk

1. Preheat the oven to 350°F. Cut parchment or wax paper to fit 2 large baking sheets that will fit side by side in your oven.

2. Pour all of the dry ingredients except the milk into a large mixing bowl and combine well with a fork. Stir in the milk and mix well. You will now have a wet dough.

3. Place one of the cut pieces of parchment or wax paper on your work surface and use your hands to flatten ¼ of the dough on the paper. Cover with plastic wrap and use a rolling pin to completely flatten the dough. It may be so thin in some places that you can see through it. Remove the plastic wrap and transfer the bran flake–covered paper onto the baking sheet.

4. Repeat the process with the second piece of parchment or wax paper and another ¼ of the dough. Bake the 2 sheets of dough for 5 minutes and then check—you want your giant bran flakes to have the consistency of a large cracker. Continue baking until the flakes have the right crispness, checking every couple of minutes so you don't burn them.

5. Let the completed flakes cool completely on the baking sheets.

6. Repeat the process with the rest of the dough.

7. Reduce the oven temperature to 275°F. Tear or break your giant flakes into normal cereal-size pieces and spread them out over the paper-covered baking sheets. Bake for 20 minutes, stirring the flakes every 5 minutes.

8. Store in an airtight container for up to 2 weeks.

Homemade Corn Flakes

Serves 3

1 cup fine or medium-fine cornmeal

¼ cup granulated or powdered sugar (optional)

water

1. Set an ungreased metal skillet over medium heat. Sift a thin layer of cornmeal into the skillet.

2. Fill a spray bottle with water and spray the cornmeal until it is moistened but not soaked.

3. Without touching the cornmeal mixture, let it cook slowly until the water is halfway evaporated; immediately sift sugar over the top, if using.

4. Cook until the water has completely evaporated and the flakes begin releasing from the bottom of the skillet. The flakes will be large.

5. Store in an airtight container for up to 2 weeks.

Hot Rice Cereal

Serves 2 to 3

1¼ cups water

1¼ cups milk

1 cup uncooked white or brown rice

½ teaspoon salt

2 to 3 teaspoons sugar or maple syrup

1 tablespoon butter or margarine (optional)

1. Mix the water and milk in a 4-quart saucepan and bring to a boil over medium heat.

2. Stir in the remaining ingredients, reduce the heat to low, and cover tightly.

3. Simmer for 20 minutes, or until the rice is tender and the liquid has been absorbed.

Wheat Berry Cereal

Serves 1

½ cup cooked wheat berries

⅛ cup chopped almonds or walnuts

½ cup fresh or dehydrated fruit

1 cup milk

Combine wheat berries, nuts, and fruit in a bowl and add milk.

Kolaches

The Czech people are famous for their pastries, and the kolache is one of their most acclaimed. The name is related to a word meaning "pocket," describing the way the fillings are tucked into the middle of a sweet roll. This versatile dough can also be fried to make donuts. Just sprinkle with powdered sugar and voilà! *Makes 20 kolaches*

¾ cup lukewarm milk

1 packet (2¼ teaspoons) active dry yeast

3 tablespoons powdered sugar

2½ tablespoons butter, melted

dash of salt

2 cups all-purpose flour (for rolling)

½ cup jelly or favorite kolache filling

1 egg yolk

1. In a bowl, add the yeast to the lukewarm milk and whisk for 1 minute. Set aside for 15 minutes.

2. In a large bowl, combine the yeast mixture along with the powdered sugar, butter, and salt. Mix for 8 minutes or until

the dough becomes smooth and no longer sticks to a wooden spoon. Cover dough and leave in a warm place to rise until doubled.

3. Preheat the oven to 400°F. Roll out the dough on floured surface to a 12 x 9-inch rectangle about ¼ inch thick. Pull off small pieces of dough, roll into 2-inch balls, and flatten into 3 to 4-inch circles. On a greased cookie sheet, place dough 2 inches apart. With the backside of a spoon, push into dough to create an indentation. Dollop a spoonful of jelly or other filling into each indentation.

4. Beat the egg yolk in a small dish and brush on the exposed dough. Bake for 15 to 20 minutes, until golden.

Rice Tortitas

This is a great recipe for leftover rice. *Serves 4 to 5*

2 cups cooked white or brown rice, cooled

3 eggs, beaten

½ cup granulated sugar

¼ teaspoon salt

1 teaspoon ground cinnamon

½ teaspoon ground nutmeg

1 teaspoon vanilla extract

2½ teaspoons baking powder

½ to 1 cup all-purpose flour

vegetable oil, for deep frying

powdered sugar for topping

1. In a large bowl, combine the cooked rice, eggs, sugar, salt, cinnamon, nutmeg, vanilla, and baking powder. Add just enough flour to hold the batter together.

2. Pour 2 to 3 inches oil into a skillet and heat over medium-high until oil begins to sizzle. Drop batter by heaping spoonfuls into the hot oil.

3. Fry until golden brown and crisp, 6 to 8 minutes.

4. Drain on paper towels and generously sprinkle with powdered sugar.

A midday meal can do wonders for renewing your energy level and keeping your metabolism active. Lunch can be anything from last night's leftovers to a simple sandwich, or it can be more substantial. Served with rolls, cornbread, or crackers, a steaming bowl of soup makes a satisfying complete meal. Typically, lunches should be between 300 and 500 calories, and they should include an array of the vitamins your body needs for proper functioning.

Beef Minestrone Soup

Serves 6 to 8

- 1 jar spaghetti meat sauce or use the recipe for Spaghetti Meat Sauce on (page 70)
- 4 cups vegetable broth
- 1 (15-ounce) can red kidney beans, undrained
- 1 (15-ounce) can small white or Great Northern beans, undrained
- ¼ cup green beans, fresh or dehydrated
- ¼ cup chopped zucchini, fresh or dehydrated
- ½ cup sliced carrots, fresh or dehydrated
- 2 tablespoons dried parsley
- 1 teaspoon dried oregano
- 1 teaspoon salt
- ½ teaspoon pepper
- ¼ teaspoon dried thyme
- 1½ cups water

⅓ cup uncooked small shell pasta

3 cups fresh baby spinach

grated Parmesan cheese, for topping (optional)

1. Pour the spaghetti sauce and vegetable broth into a large stockpot. Add the canned beans, vegetables, seasonings, and water.

2. Bring the soup to a boil over medium-high heat, then reduce the heat to low and allow to simmer uncovered for 20 minutes.

3. When almost ready to serve, add the pasta and cook for an additional 20 minutes, or until the soup has the desired consistency.

4. Ladle the soup into bowls and stir in fresh spinach. Top the individual servings with Parmesan cheese, if desired.

Vegetarian Chili

Adding 2 cups of wheat berries can add carbohydrates and boost this meal's nutrition. *Serves 3*

1 (15.4-ounce) can black beans

1 (15.4-ounce) can red kidney beans

1 (15.4-ounce) can whole kernel corn

1 (14.5-ounce) can diced tomatoes

1 (14.5-ounce) can crushed tomatoes

¼ cup dehydrated green bell peppers

2 tablespoons dried onion flakes

2 tablespoons chili powder

1 tablespoon garlic powder

hot sauce, to taste

1. Rinse and drain the beans and corn. Place in a large saucepan.

2. Stir in all the remaining ingredients except the hot sauce.

3. Bring to a boil over medium heat, then reduce the heat to low and simmer for at least 30 minutes, until the flavors are well blended.

4. Add hot sauce to taste.

Sweet Potato Chili

Serves 4 to 6

1 sweet potato or yam, peeled and cubed or 1 (15-ounce) can sweet potatoes, drained

1 onion, diced

1 bell pepper, diced

1 apple, peeled, cored, and cubed

4 garlic cloves, minced

1 (28-ounce) can diced tomatoes, undrained

1 (15.5-ounce) can black beans, undrained

1 (15.5-ounce) can navy beans, undrained

1 cup water

1 tablespoon ground cumin

1 tablespoon chili powder

1 teaspoon unsweetened cocoa powder

¼ teaspoon ground cinnamon

salt and pepper

1 (12.5-ounce) can of chunk chicken breast (optional)

hot sauce

In a large pot, combine all the ingredients except the hot sauce along with the liquid in cans. Bring to a boil over medium heat, then reduce the heat and simmer, uncovered, for at least 30 minutes, until the flavors are well blended. Stir in hot sauce to taste.

Baked-Bean Chili

Serves 4 to 5

1 pound ground beef (or other ground meat) or 1 cup freeze-dried beef or 4 cups dehydrated beef

2 (15.5-ounce) cans baked beans

1 (14.5-ounce) can diced or stewed

¼ cup barbecue sauce

¼ cup packed brown sugar

3 tablespoons chili powder

1 tablespoon onion powder

1 tablespoon garlic powder

salt, to taste

1. Rehydrate any dehydrated meat for 1 hour. Combine all the ingredients in a large pot and bring to a boil over medium heat. If cooking ground beef, brown meat in a skillet, breaking up ground meat with a spoon.

2. Reduce the heat to low, cover, and simmer for 1½ hours, stirring frequently to ensure the beans do not get scorched (or until the ground meat is thoroughly cooked, if using fresh meat).

3. Remove the lid and simmer for another 30 minutes.

3-Can Black Bean Soup

Serves 4

1 (15-ounce) can whole kernel corn, undrained

1 (15-ounce) can black beans, undrained

1 (28-ounce) can diced tomatoes, undrained

1 tablespoon chili powder

3 teaspoons garlic powder

¼ teaspoon cayenne pepper

1 tablespoon dried onion flakes

2 tablespoons chicken bouillon granules

1 tablespoon dried parsley

salt and black pepper, to taste

cilantro, coarsely chopped (optional)

tortilla chips or baked flour tortilla crisps

1. Pour the corn, beans, and tomatoes into a 16-quart stockpot along with the can liquids.

2. Stir in the following 7 ingredients (chili powder through salt and pepper).

3. Bring the mixture to a boil over medium heat, then reduce the heat to low and simmer, uncovered, for 20 to 30 minutes.

4. Stir in cilantro to taste, if desired. Ladle the hot soup into bowls and top with crumbled tortilla chips or crisps to serve.

Creamy Corn Chowder

Serves 2 to 3

1 (15-ounce) can whole kernel corn, drained and rinsed

1 (15-ounce) can creamed corn, undrained

2 cups milk or ⅔ cup instant nonfat milk mixed with 2 cups water

⅔ cup instant mashed potato flakes, or as needed

salt and pepper

1. In a 4-quart saucepan, combine both kinds of corn and the milk.

Bring to a boil over medium heat, then reduce the heat to low and simmer, uncovered, for 5 minutes.

2. Stir in the instant mashed potato flakes, a little bit at a time, until the chowder is as thick as you want it.

3. Season to taste with salt and pepper.

Split Pea Soup

Serves 4 to 6

1 pound split peas

5 cups water or vegetable broth, or more as needed

1½ cups diced carrots or 1 (15-ounce) can carrots or 1 cup diced dehydrated carrots

2 tablespoons olive or vegetable oil

3 tablespoons dried onion flakes

2 cups diced ham (smoked, canned, or dehydrated)

1 tablespoon seasoning salt

2 bay leaves

1 tablespoon dried thyme

pepper, to taste

1. Rinse and sort the peas to remove any dirt or stones.

2. Combine all the ingredients in a 4-quart saucepan. Bring to a boil over medium heat.

3. Reduce the heat and simmer the soup, uncovered, for 2 hours, or until the peas have disintegrated, stirring frequently and add water if needed.

4. Remove the pot from the heat and let the soup stand for 15 minutes to thicken. Remove and discard the bay leaves before serving the soup.

Leftover Chowder

Serves 8

1 leftover cooked chicken carcass

8 cups water

5 bacon strips, cooked and chopped

2 garlic cloves, minced

2 onions, diced

2 medium red potatoes, peeled and diced

4 carrots, peeled and sliced or 2 cups sliced dehydrated carrots

kernels from 2 ears of corn or 2 cups dehydrated corn kernels

1½ teaspoons prepared Cajun seasoning, or use the recipe on page 22

1 mild or spicy chile, diced (optional)

2 tablespoons all-purpose flour

milk or heavy cream, for serving (optional)

1. In a covered large stockpot over low heat, simmer the chicken carcass in the water for 7 hours. Add more water if needed.

2. Lift out the chicken and allow it to cool. Strain the broth through a sieve into 16-quart stockpot; discard the bones, skin, and other remnants.

3. When the chicken is cool enough to handle, pick any remaining meat off the bones.

4. Add the chicken meat to the broth along with all the remaining ingredients except the flour and milk. Allow the

chowder to simmer actively over medium heat for 15 to 25 minutes, or until the vegetables are soft.

5. To thicken the soup, whisk 1 cup of the broth together with 2 tablespoons of flour in a medium bowl. Stir into the chowder.

6. To make the soup creamy, pour a splash of milk or cream into the individual bowls before ladling in the chowder.

Cream of Asparagus Soup

Serves 3

2 (10.5-ounce) cans asparagus

4 cups milk or 1½ cups instant nonfat dry milk mixed with 4 cups chicken broth or water

2 chicken bouillon cubes (if not using broth)

1 tablespoon garlic powder

1½ teaspoons dried thyme

1. Using a blender, purée the asparagus with the liquid from the cans. Alternatively, use a potato masher to produce the consistency you want.

2. Transfer the puréed asparagus to a 4-quart saucepan and stir in the milk or dry milk mixture. Add the bouillon (if using), garlic powder, and thyme; blend well.

3. Over medium heat, bring the soup to a low simmer. Simmer until heated through.

Potato Cheese Soup

Serves 3

1 (15.4-ounce) can condensed cheese soup

⅔ cup nonfat dry milk

1 cup water

1¼ cups instant mashed potato flakes

1 tablespoon onion powder

salt and pepper

freeze-dried or dried chives, to taste

2 tablespoons bacon bits (optional)

1. Combine the canned soup, dry milk, and water in a 9-quart saucepan over medium heat. Bring to a simmer, but do boil. Let simmer for 5 minutes.

2. Stir in the potato flakes, onion powder, salt, and pepper, mixing well. Continue to simmer until heated through.

3. Top individual bowls of hot soup with chives and bacon bits, as desired.

Dr. Mom Chicken Noodle Soup

Leave the skin on the onion to create a golden brown broth. *Serves 6*

2 (14.5-ounce) cans chicken broth or 4 cups hot water mixed with 2 chicken bouillon cubes

2 (12.5-ounce) cans chunk chicken

2 tablespoons dried garlic flakes or 6 garlic cloves, minced

2 tablespoons dried minced onion or 1 whole onion, chopped

2 tablespoons dried parsley

1 tablespoon dried oregano

1 (15.4-ounce) can peas and carrots, drained

½ (12-ounce) package egg noodles

1. Combine the first 6 ingredients in a large saucepan over medium heat.

2. Simmer, uncovered for 1 to 2 hours to allow flavors to meld.

3. Add the drained peas and carrots and the egg noodles. Bring to a low boil and cook as long as the package directs for al dente noodles.

Vegetable Beef and Barley Soup

Serves 6

1 pound ground or cubed beef, 1 cup dehydrated beef or 12 ounces dried beef

1 (12–ounce) can V8 or tomato juice

1 (15-ounce) can peas and carrots, undrained

1 (15-ounce) can whole kernel corn, undrained

1 (15-ounce) can green beans, undrained

1 (15-ounce) can white or red kidney beans, undrained

½ cup uncooked pearl barley

2 bay leaves

1 tablespoon dried minced garlic

1 tablespoon dried onion flakes

½ teaspoon dried marjoram

½ teaspoon chili powder

½ teaspoon dried thyme

salt and pepper

1. If you are using dehydrated ground beef, rehydrate in water for 30 minutes before adding to a large pot. If you are using ground or cubed beef, brown it in a skillet, breaking up the ground beef with a spoon. When browned, drain the grease.

2. In a large stockpot, combine the beef with all the remaining ingredients.

3. Bring to a boil over medium heat, then reduce to a low simmer and cook for 2 hours, covered, until the beef is completely cooked and the barley is tender. Stir often during the cooking process.

Lucky Bean Soup Recipe

Serves 8

1 pound Hearty Bean Soup Mix (page 83)

1 (28-ounce) can diced tomatoes

1 medium onion, chopped

½ cup chopped green bell pepper

½ cup chopped celery

1 or 2 garlic cloves, chopped

1 tablespoon chili powder

½ teaspoon ground cumin

10 to 12 cups water, or as needed

1 pound smoked sausage or ham

salt and pepper

1. Rinse the beans and cover with water to soak overnight, or at least 12 hours. Drain.

2. In a 9-quart stockpot, combine everything except the sausage or ham, salt, and pepper. The water should cover the other ingredients. Bring to a boil over medium-high heat.

3. Reduce the heat and simmer for 1 to 2 hours, uncovered, until the beans are tender. Add the sausage or ham and season to taste with salt and pepper. Cook until the flavor of the meat is well blended into the beans.

Potato Soup

Serves 4

2 tablespoons chopped dehydrated green onions

2 tablespoons chopped dehydrated celery

2 tablespoons butter or margarine

4 cups milk, or as needed

4 servings instant potato flakes

½ teaspoon chicken bouillon granules

salt

¼ teaspoon pepper

dash of garlic powder

paprika, parsley, bacon bits, or grated cheese, for garnish (optional)

1. In a 4-quart saucepan over high heat, rehydrate the onion and celery in ¾ cups boiling water for 5 minutes.

2. Over low heat, sauté the rehydrated onion and celery in the butter or margarine.

3. Add the milk, potato flakes, bouillon, salt, pepper, and garlic powder. Heat to almost boiling, stirring constantly. If the soup seems too thick, thin with more milk or with water.

4. Remove from the heat. Garnish individual servings with paprika, parsley, bacon bits, or grated cheese, if you wish.

Taco Soup

This soup is good served over rice or tortilla chips. *Serves 4*

- 2 cups dehydrated or fresh ground beef, cooked
- 1 onion, chopped
- 1 (15.5-ounce) can kidney or black beans
- 1 (15.5-ounce) can pinto beans
- 2 (28-ounce) cans stewed tomatoes
- 1 (10-ounce) can Rotel diced tomatoes and green chiles
- 1 (1.5-ounce) packet taco seasoning
- 1 (1.5-ounce) packet ranch dressing mix
- 1 to 2 cups water

Without draining the cans, pour all the ingredients into a large saucepan or stockpot. Stir to combine. Simmer over medium heat, covered, for 30 minutes.

Goulash

Serves 5

- ¼ cup vegetable oil
- 1 pound bone-in pork or beef
- ½ cup dried onion flakes or 1 whole onion, sliced
- 1 teaspoon dried garlic flakes or 2 garlic cloves, minced
- 2 tablespoons paprika
- 3 to 5 cups prepared sauerkraut
- 3 cups water
- salt and pepper
- sour cream, for serving (optional)

1. Heat the oil in a large pot over medium-high heat. When the oil is sizzling, add the meat and sear 4 to 5 minutes on each side.

2. Reduce the heat to medium and add the onions, garlic, and paprika and continue cooking until the meat is cooked, 20 to 30 minutes. Remove the meat to a cutting board.

3. Scrape up the browned bits from the bottom of the pot. Add the sauerkraut and water and bring to a simmer over medium heat.

4. When the meat has cooled enough to handle, cut it into cubes and return it to the pot. For the richest flavor, add the meat bones, too. Season to taste with salt and pepper. Simmer on low heat, uncovered, for 1 to 2 hours.

5. Top with sour cream to serve, if you wish.

USE YOUR NOODLE!

Ramen noodles are a prepper favorite. Those little cubes of ultra-cheap carbohydrates are a mainstay in many preppers' pantries! They are inexpensive and quick to prepare, and they add some easy-to-digest carbs to a meal for extra energy. But the just-add-water packets will get dull very quickly. Here are some ideas for pumping up your basic ramen noodles. Try these additions to cooked, unflavored ramen noodles, in whatever proportions you like.

1. Chives, canned baby corn (drained), soy sauce, Oriental seasoning packet

2. Marinara sauce, grated Parmesan cheese, beef seasoning packet

3. Condensed cream of chicken soup, canned mixed vegetables (drained), chicken seasoning packet

4. Prepared macaroni and cheese dinner, grated Parmesan cheese, vegetable seasoning packet

5. Diced pineapple (drained), diced canned ham, dried bell pepper, Oriental seasoning packet

6. 1 (15.5-ounce) can of green beans (drained), 1 (15.5-ounce) can of kidney beans (drained), (15.5-ounce) can of lima beans (drained), Italian salad dressing (serve cold or at room temperature)

7. Condensed tomato soup, Tabasco sauce, shredded cheese (optional)

8. Coca-cola, salted peanuts (chopped), thinly sliced beef jerky, beef seasoning packet

9. Creamy peanut butter (1 to 2 tablespoons per noodle pack), chives, Oriental seasoning packet

10. Canned chili, Tabasco sauce, Cheez Whiz, beef seasoning packet

11. Drained canned tuna, Italian salad dressing, vegetable seasoning packet

12. Salsa, sliced pepperette, pickle relish, yellow mustard

13. Lemon juice, garlic powder, Parmesan cheese, vegetable seasoning packet

14. Diced Spam, green peas, garlic powder, pork seasoning packet

15. Extra water, canned mixed vegetables, undrained canned kidney beans, undrained beef seasoning packet

Thermos noodles: Try this quick, low-fuel idea for preparing your noodles in the event of a blackout or limited fuel. Use 1 cup water for noodles, 2 cups water for soup.

Crunch up the package of noodles, then open one end and dump the noodles into a wide-mouth thermos. Sprinkle the seasoning packet on top. Add boiling or hot water and cap the thermos for 5 minutes—no longer, or they'll be mush! Voilà—perfect noodles!

Pantry Chicken and Dumplings

Serves 6 to 8

2¼ cups biscuit mix (such as Bisquick)

⅔ cup milk or ⅔ cup water mixed with ½ cup nonfat dry milk

2 (12.5-ounce) cans chunk chicken

2 (14-ounce) cans chicken broth or 4 cups water mixed with 2 chicken bouillon cubes

1 tablespoon dried parsley

1 tablespoon garlic powder

1 tablespoon onion powder

salt and pepper

1. In a medium mixing bowl, combine the biscuit mix and the milk to make the dumpling dough.

2. Place the chicken, broth, and seasonings in a 9-quart stockpot and bring to a boil over medium-high heat.

3. While the broth is coming to a boil, flatten out the dough about ¼ inch thick on a cutting board. Once the soup is boiling, tear off medium-sized pieces of dough and drop them into the liquid.

4. After 1 minute, stir very gently to make sure all the dumplings are completely moistened. Reduce the heat, cover, and simmer for 10 minutes.

Asian Ramen Salad

For a heartier meal, add 1 cup cooked chicken to this salad. *Serves 6*

DRESSING

⅓ cup peanut butter

⅓ cup water

½ teaspoon garlic powder

1 tablespoon soy sauce

2 tablespoons sesame seed oil

2 tablespoons apple cider vinegar

salt and pepper

NOODLES

2 (3-ounce) packages ramen noodles, broken up, spice packet discarded

½ head cabbage, shredded

1 cup diced celery

¼ cup chopped onion

¼ cup diced carrots

¼ cup roasted, salted peanuts

4 tablespoons fresh cilantro or 2 tablespoons dried cilantro

salt and pepper

1. In a small bowl, whisk together all the dressing ingredients. Set aside.

2. Cook the ramen noodles according to the package directions. (Do not add the spice packet.) Drain.

3. In a large mixing bowl, combine the cooked noodles with the remaining salad ingredients. Gently toss with the dressing. Serve immediately.

Southern Chicken Salad

Serves 4

1 (12.5-ounce) can chunk chicken or 1 cup chopped cooked chicken

¼ cup cashews, pecans, or walnuts

2 tablespoons finely diced yellow onion or 1 tablespoon rehydrated diced onion

½ cup finely diced red apple

¼ cup dried cranberries, blueberries, or other berries

¼ cup diced purple grapes

¼ cup mayonnaise

½ teaspoon curry powder

salt

Mix all the ingredients well. Use on crackers, in salads, or as a sandwich filling.

Garden Tuna Salad

Serves 3 to 4

1 (5-ounce) can tuna, drained

2 hard-cooked eggs, shredded

1 large dill pickle, finely diced

¼ cup minced yellow onion

¼ cup mayonnaise

½ teaspoon lemon pepper seasoning

salt and pepper

Mix all the ingredients well. Use on crackers, in salads, or as a sandwich filling.

Spicy Tuna Salad

Serves 3 to 4

1 (5-ounce) can tuna, drained

¼ cup mayonnaise

1 teaspoon chili powder

1 teaspoon lemon pepper seasoning

⅛ teaspoon garlic powder

dash of cayenne pepper

1 teaspoon peach jelly

salt and pepper

Mix all the ingredients well. Use on crackers, in salads, or as a sandwich filling.

Deviled Ham Salad

Serves 3 to 4

1 (4.25-ounce) can deviled ham

1 large dill pickle, finely diced

1½ tablespoons finely diced jalapeño chiles

3 tablespoons mayonnaise

½ teaspoon dry mustard

¼ teaspoon onion powder

salt and pepper

Mix all the ingredients well. Use on crackers, in salads, or as a sandwich filling.

Egg Salad

Serves 3 to 4

6 hard-cooked eggs

½ cup mayonnaise

1 teaspoon dry mustard

1 tablespoon sweet pickle relish

dash of cayenne pepper

salt and pepper

Using a cheese grater, shred the eggs. Combine with the remaining ingredients, mixing well. Use on crackers, in salads, or as a sandwich filling.

Chicken Rice Salad

Serves 4

1 (12.5-ounce) can chunk chicken, drained

2 cups cooked white rice

3 cups chopped lettuce, spinach, or sprouts

2 teaspoons ground cumin

1 tablespoon lemon juice

2 teaspoons lemon pepper seasoning

Mix all the ingredients together and serve immediately.

Chicken Macaroni Salad

Serves 4

2 cups cooked macaroni

1 (12.5-ounce) can chunk chicken, drained

½ cup mayonnaise, or as needed

¼ cup onion, chopped

¼ cup celery, chopped

¼ cup sweet pickle relish

2 teaspoons granulated sugar

2 teaspoons white vinegar

½ teaspoon prepared yellow mustard

salt and pepper

Combine all the ingredients in a large bowl and stir well. Add a little more mayonnaise, if necessary. Taste and adjust the seasonings as needed. Cover and chill for several hours before serving.

Pasta Italiano

Serves 4

2 cups cooked pasta

1 (3.25-ounce) can pitted black olives, drained and sliced

½ fresh or dehydrated red bell pepper, diced

¼ cup coarsely chopped dehydrated tomatoes

2 tablespoons fresh finely chopped red onion

½ cup mayonnaise

2 tablespoons prepared Italian salad dressing

2 tablespoons lemon juice

2 tablespoons dried basil

1 tablespoon dried parsley

¼ teaspoon pepper

½ teaspoon salt, or to taste

Combine all the ingredients in a medium bowl and stir well. Add a little more mayonnaise, if necessary. Taste and adjust the seasonings as needed. Cover and chill for several hours before serving.

Ham and Pea Salad

Serves 6

4 cups cooked macaroni pasta

1 cup thinly sliced celery

1 cup diced onion

1 cup diced ham

1½ cups frozen green peas, thawed

¼ cup mayonnaise

½ cup prepared ranch dressing

1 teaspoon dried basil

dash of garlic powder

salt and pepper

Combine all the ingredients in a large bowl and stir well. Add a little more mayonnaise, if necessary. Taste and adjust the seasonings as needed. Cover and chill for several hours before serving.

Momma's Fish Patties

Serves 4 to 5

1 (16-ounce) can salmon or other fish

½ cup saltine cracker crumbs or cornmeal

¼ cup cornmeal

2 eggs, lightly beaten

¼ teaspoon salt

¼ teaspoon pepper

dash of Tabasco sauce

vegetable oil for frying

1. Drain the juices from the canned fish; reserve.

2. Flake the fish, making sure that all the skin and bones have been removed.

3. Combine the cracker crumbs with the reserved fish liquid. Allow to stand for 5 minutes, or until the liquid has been absorbed. Stir in the flaked fish, cornmeal, eggs, salt, pepper, and Tabasco. Shape the fish mixture into patties.

4. Pour oil into a heavy skillet to a depth of ¼ inch. Heat the oil over medium heat. Fry the patties 2 to 3 minutes on each side in the hot oil until browned. Drain on paper towels and serve warm.

Tuscan Bean Salad

Serves 6

2 (15.4-ounce) cans navy beans or cannellini beans, drained

1 (6-ounce) can pitted black olives, chopped

1 small onion, chopped, or ½ cup chopped dehydrated onion, rehydrated

¼ cup dehydrated chopped tomatoes

¼ cup olive oil

2 tablespoons balsamic vinegar

2 cups coarsely chopped fresh spinach

1 tablespoon Italian seasoning

dash of cayenne pepper

salt and pepper

Combine all the ingredients in a medium bowl and stir well. Add a little more mayonnaise, if necessary. Taste and adjust the seasonings as needed. Cover and chill for several hours before serving.

Bean Patties

Serve these patties hot with warm flatbread or as a sandwich filling.

Serves 6 medium or 12 small patties

1 (15.5-ounce) can beans (such as chickpeas, lentils, black, or pinto beans), drained

1 large onion, finely chopped

2 garlic cloves, finely chopped

1 teaspoon ground cumin

3 tablespoons chopped dried fresh parsley

3 tablespoons chopped dehydrated tomatoes, rehydrated

2 teaspoons chili powder

2 tablespoons cornmeal

salt and pepper

1 tablespoon all-purpose flour

vegetable oil for frying

1. In a medium bowl, combine the beans, onion, garlic, cumin, parsley, tomatoes, chili powder, cornmeal, salt, and pepper. Mix well. Stir in the flour.

2. Mash the beans, mixing the ingredients well. You can also combine the ingredients in a food processor. You want the result to be a thick paste.

3. Form the mixture into balls about the size of ping-pong balls. Flatten slightly.

4. In a deep skillet, heat 2 inches of oil until it sizzles when a drop of water hits oil. Fry the patties in the hot oil until sides are golden brown, turning every 5 to 7 minutes. Drain on a paper towel and serve warm.

Chicken Bean Wraps

To make a crispier version, brush a small amount of oil on both sides of the tortillas and crisp in a 345°F oven for 5 minutes, or until the tortillas are as crisp as desired. *Serves 4 to 5*

1 (16-ounce) can refried beans

dash of chili powder

4 or 5 flour tortillas

1 (12.5-ounce) can chunk chicken, drained

shredded lettuce or sprouts

1 cup prepared salsa (page 67)

shredded sharp Cheddar cheese (optional)

Recipe variation: Use 1 cup ground beef crumbles instead of chicken.

1. On low heat, in a small pot, heat refried beans with the chili powder until they reach desired temperature. In a skillet, heat and warm tortillas 30 seconds on each side. Slather the warm tortillas with refried beans.

2. Top each tortilla with chicken chunks, lettuce or sprouts, salsa, and cheese, if using.

6 SUPPER

It's all well and good to have a cookbook full of recipes, but this cookbook is for the prepper. We always have not only Plan A, but also Plans B, C, and sometimes even D. Cooking from the storage pantry goes hand in hand with the prepper lifestyle. Fresh ingredients may not be available, but that doesn't mean we can't make our favorite comforting recipes. Be flexible—don't say, "I can't make that because I don't have all the ingredients." Be creative and think not just about Plan B, but about Ingredient B!

In many families, dinner is the only meal of the day at which everyone is present. For that reason, lots of us choose to make it the most delicious and comforting meal possible. The recipes in

this chapter bring to mind a cozy warm country kitchen, and no one will ever guess that nearly all the ingredients are straight from your prepper's pantry! Keep in mind that on average, dinner should consist of 30% of your daily calories, or between 500 and 800 calories.

Use the following chart as a jumping-off point for devising your own Plan B. When fresh ingredients are scarce, the suggested substitutions can be used for the recipes in this book and for your own familiar favorites.

FRESH INGREDIENT	SUBSTITUTION
Apples	Dehydrated apple slices, applesauce
Beef	Freeze-dried ground beef, freeze-dried sliced beef, dehydrated beef crumbles, canned beef, chipped beef, beef pouches, TVP, jerky
Bell peppers	Dehydrated peppers, freeze-dried peppers
Butter	Canned butter, freeze-dried butter powder, shortening
Carrots	Dehydrated carrots, freeze-dried carrots
Celery	Dehydrated celery, freeze-dried celery
Cheese	Freeze-dried shredded cheese, Cheez Whiz, Velveeta processed cheese, canned cheese soup
Chicken	Canned or chunk chicken, freeze-dried chicken, dehydrated chicken pieces
Eggs	Freeze-dried powdered eggs, 1 tablespoon soy flour plus 1 tablespoon water, 1 tablespoon applesauce
Ham	Canned flaked ham, Spam, canned ham, freeze-dried ham, dehydrated ham bits
Milk	Nonfat dry powdered milk, nonfat dry milk, freeze-dried milk powder, canned evaporated milk
Mushrooms	Canned mushrooms, freeze-dried mushrooms, dehydrated mushrooms
Onions	Onion powder, freeze-dried onion, dehydrated onion, onion soup mix
Turkey	Canned flaked turkey, freeze-dried turkey, dehydrated turkey pieces
Sausage	Freeze-dried sausage crumbles, pepperettes, or little smokies

A NOTE ABOUT FREEZE-DRIED FOODS

Freeze-dried foods can be a great addition to any prepper's pantry. The beauty of freeze-dried food isn't just the nutrition and variety it can add to your family's diet, but that it can last 25 years or more. Foods that would normally be off limits during a disaster can be neatly lined up on your shelves, awaiting the addition of hot water to provide a burst of vitamins, minerals, and flavor.

Learn in good times to reconstitute freeze-dried foods and use them in your normal recipes—it will totally change your outlook toward surviving with the contents of your pantry!

Meats—Investing in freeze-dried meats will allow you to make all your normal recipes with only slight adaptations. Try these in freeze-dried form:

- Chicken breast
- Turkey breast
- Ground beef
- Beef strips
- Sausage crumbles
- Ham

Vegetables—Some veggies that you can't get in cans are available in freeze-dried form. Bell pepper, for example, might be hard to find in the middle of a winter blackout. But if you have a well-stocked section of freeze-dried foods, a scoop of peppers will be at your fingertips. Some useful freeze-dried vegetables:

- Broccoli
- Cauliflower
- Celery
- Diced carrots
- Green bell peppers
- Mushrooms
- Onions
- Spinach
- Zucchini

Eggs and dairy products—These may be lacking in your pantry, since they need to be refrigerated or frozen. However, freeze-dried foods will let you add cheesy good-ness to casseroles or enjoy a hot breakfast omelet. How great would it be to be able to make your kids a Friday-night pizza in the midst of a grid-down situation? Think about stocking up on #10 cans of the following:

Shredded Cheddar and mozzarella cheeses

- Powdered cheese
- Powdered milk, buttermilk
- Powdered whole eggs, egg whites, and egg yolks
- Powdered butter
- Powdered shortening

Tater Skins

This has become an American favorite. *Serves 8*

6 medium russet or Idaho potatoes, scrubbed (about 7 pounds)

olive oil, as needed

1 cup chopped bacon or ham

salt and pepper

½ cup shredded fresh or freeze-dried Cheddar cheese

sour cream or yogurt, for dipping (optional)

3 green onions, finely chopped

1. Preheat the oven to 400°F. Rub the potatoes with olive oil and bake 30 minutes. (To conserve fuel, do this while you're cooking something else.)

2. Cook the bacon or ham in a skillet until crispy, then drain on a paper towel.

3. Slice the baked potatoes in half and scoop out the centers until there is only ½ inch of potato flesh left on the skin. Reserve the scooped-out flesh for another use.

4. Increase the oven temperature to 450°F.

5. Rub the potato skins inside and out with olive oil and sprinkle with salt and pepper.

6. Spread the potato skins on a baking sheet and cook for 10 minutes on one side, then turn them over and cook for another 10 minutes, until crisp and lightly browned.

7. Remove the potatoes and set the oven on broil. Arrange the potatoes skin-side down and

sprinkle with the cheese and cooked bacon or ham. Return them to the oven and broil for 2 minutes.

8. To serve, top with sour cream or yogurt (if using) and the chopped green onions.

Potato Dumplings

Serve these dumplings with hot soup or a hearty stew. *Serves 8*

2 whole russet potatoes (about 2 pounds), cooked and mashed

1 teaspoon salt, plus salt for cooking water

1 cup all-purpose flour, plus more for rolling

2 eggs, lightly beaten

lukewarm water, as needed

3 tablespoons butter, optional

1. In a medium bowl, mash the cooked potatoes until smooth.

2. Bring a large pot of salted water to a boil over high heat while you prepare the dumplings.

3. In a large bowl, combine salt, flour, and eggs. If the dough seems too dry, add 1 or 2 tablespoons lukewarm water. Add potatoes and mix everything together to make a smooth, medium-thick dough.

4. Place the dough on a lightly floured surface and knead the mixture until smooth. Add 1 tablespoon flour if dough is sticky. Divide the dough in half. With floured hands, shape the dough into 1½-inch balls.

5. Carefully transfer the dough pieces into the boiling water. Reduce the heat to medium, cover the pot, and cook for 10 to 15 minutes or until dumplings rise to the surface. If the dumplings stick to the bottom of the pot, use a wooden spoon or a spatula to unstick them. Drain in a colander. Drizzle with melted butter, if preferred.

6. Use a slotted spoon to lift the dumplings out of the water and allow to dry for a few minutes on a paper towel–lined plate and then turn over to dry the other side.

Dottie's Easy Chicken Pot Pie

Serves 4 to 5

1 Basic Pie Crust recipe (page 187)

1 (12.5-ounce) can chunk white chicken, drained

1 (15-ounce) can mixed vegetables, drained

1 (10-ounce) can condensed cream of mushroom soup

salt and pepper

THE TASTY TATER

The humble baked potato is a fine, filling, and inexpensive base for a variety of budget-saving meals. If you are heating off-grid with a wood stove, fireplace, or campfire, you can wrap potatoes in heavy-duty foil and bake them in the embers, using no additional fuel. Or they can be wrapped in foil and tossed into the oven alongside your main dish, to have at that meal or later.

A potato is only plain until you top it! Try these pantry items to top your taters:

1. Canned chili
2. Condensed cheese soup with chives and chopped ham, Spam, or bacon
3. Salsa
4. Reconstituted freeze-dried sour cream and chives
5. Homemade plain yogurt, garlic powder, and seasoning salt
6. Butter flakes and dried dill
7. Canned flaked ham and Cheez Whiz
8. Baked beans and sausage crumbles
9. Tuna, mayonnaise, and corn
10. Leftover spaghetti sauce with meat
11. Yogurt, curry powder, and green peas
12. Leftover meat and gravy
13. Bacon, mayonnaise, and diced pineapple
14. Mushrooms and gravy, with optional cheese topping
15. Pizza sauce, green peppers, mushrooms, onions, chopped pepperettes, and cheese
16. Refried beans and salsa
17. Pesto
18. Leftover chopped roasted veggies
19. Roasted red peppers, roasted garlic, and a drizzle of olive oil
20. Hummus and Greek seasoning
21. Fajita filling
22. Seasoned ground beef
23. Ground beef, mushrooms, and condensed cream of mushroom soup
24. Marinated artichoke hearts and roasted red peppers
25. Smoked sausage and sauerkraut

1. Prepare the pastry dough, wrap in plastic, and refrigerate at least 30 minutes.
2. Preheat the oven to 350°F.
3. Divide the pie dough in half. On a floured surface, use a floured rolling pin to roll half of the dough to a 12-inch round. Transfer it into a 9-inch pie pan, letting the edges hang over.
4. In a large bowl, mix together the chicken, vegetables, and mushroom soup. Season with salt and pepper to taste. Pour the mixture into the pie shell.

5. Roll the rest of the dough to an 11-inch round. Carefully transfer the dough round onto the pie. Trim the edges to ½ inch, fold under, press together, and crimp. Slit the top to make steam vents.

6. Bake until the crust is golden brown, 40 to 45 minutes.

Shepherd's Pie

Serves 3 to 4

1 pound ground beef, cooked and crumbled or 4 cups dehydrated beef crumbles

1 (10-ounce) can condensed cream of mushroom soup

1 (10-ounce) can creamed corn

1 (10-ounce) can peas and carrots, drained

½ teaspoon dried thyme

1 tablespoon dried minced onion

1 tablespoon dried garlic flakes

salt and pepper

⅔ cup instant potato flakes, reconstituted according to the package directions

2 tablespoons butter, melted (optional)

1. Preheat the oven to 375°F. Lightly grease a 1.8-liter casserole or baking dish.

2. Combine everything except for the potato mixture and butter in the prepared dish, mixing well.

3. Top with the potato mixture and brush with butter, if using.

4. Bake, uncovered, for 40 minutes, until lightly golden and heated through.

Creamed Tuna

Serves 3 to 4

¼ cup diced onions

2 tablespoons butter

1 tablespoon all-purpose flour

½ teaspoon salt

⅛ teaspoon freshly ground pepper

1 cup milk

1 (5-ounce) can tuna, drained

1 (10-ounce) can peas, drained

toast or cooked rice, for serving

1. In a medium saucepan over medium-high heat, sauté the onions in the butter until tender but not browned. Stir in the flour, salt, and pepper.

2. Add the milk all at once; cook, stirring constantly, until the mixture thickens and bubbles.

3. Break up the tuna with a fork, and add the tuna and peas

to the creamed mixture and simmer for 5 minutes.

4. To serve, spoon over toast or rice.

Scalloped Potatoes and Ham

Serves 4 to 6

6 medium potatoes, peeled and thinly sliced (about 4 to 6 pounds)

1½ cups chopped ham (fully cooked or dehydrated)

1 cup sliced carrots (fresh or dehydrated)

½ cup peas (fresh or dehydrated)

1 teaspoon dehydrated minced garlic or 1 garlic clove, minced

3 tablespoons chopped dehydrated onion or 1 medium onion, chopped

2 (10-ounce) cans condensed cream of mushroom soup

½ cup unsweetened condensed milk

salt and pepper

1. Preheat the oven to 350°F. Lightly grease a 1½ to 2-quart casserole dish.

2. Place a layer of potatoes in the bottom of the dish. Add a layer of ham and then sprinkle on a layer of carrots, peas, garlic, and onion. Continue to alternate layers until all the potatoes, ham, and vegetables have been used.

3. In a large bowl, stir together the mushroom soup, condensed milk, salt, and pepper. Pour over the layered ingredients in the casserole dish.

4. Cover and bake for 1 hour, until the potatoes are tender.

Tuna Noodle Casserole

Serves 3 to 4

1 (10-ounce) can tuna, drained well

1 (10-ounce) can condensed cream of mushroom soup or other condensed cream of vegetable soup

1 (15-ounce) can peas, drained

½ (12-ounce) package egg noodles, cooked and drained

½ to 1 cup French-fried onions or ½ cup fine breadcrumbs

1. Preheat the oven to 400°F. Lightly grease a medium 1.8-liter casserole dish.

2. Mix the tuna, soup, and peas in the prepared dish until well combined. Gently stir in the cooked noodles.

3. Top with the French-fried onions or breadcrumbs.

4. Bake, uncovered, for 30 minutes, or until lightly browned.

Reuben Casserole

Serves 2 to 3

1 (15-ounce) can corned beef, chopped

1 (10-ounce) can condensed cream of mushroom soup

1 (12-ounce) jar sauerkraut

1 (12-ounce) package egg noodles, cooked and drained

1 cup shredded mozzarella or Swiss cheese (optional)

1. Preheat the oven to 325°F. Lightly grease a medium 1.8-liter casserole dish.

2. Mix all the ingredients together in the prepared dish.

3. Bake for 45 minutes, or until the top is lightly browned.

Chicken with Lemon Basil Sauce

Serves 4 to 6

3 tablespoons olive oil, divided

1 tablespoon distilled white vinegar

¼ (.4-ounce) packet ranch dressing mix (optional)

pasta, cooked al dente

2 (12.5-ounce) cans chunk chicken, drained

2 garlic cloves, chopped

2 tablespoons fresh lemon juice

1 teaspoon grated lemon zest

1 cup low-salt chicken broth

1 cup spinach (canned, fresh, or dehydrated)

½ cup chopped fresh basil or 1 tablespoon dried basil

salt

pepper

1. In a small bowl, make a sauce for the pasta by whisking together 1 tablespoon of the oil, the vinegar, and the ranch dressing mix (if using). Add to the cooked pasta and stir to combine. Set aside.

2. Heat the remaining 2 tablespoons olive oil in a wide, heavy skillet over medium-high heat. Add the chicken and sauté until browned. Add the chicken to the bowl of pasta. Leave the juices in the pan.

3. In same skillet, reduce heat to medium, add the garlic to the pan and sauté for 2 minutes. Add the lemon juice and lemon zest. Stir until well blended. Add the chicken broth and spinach; simmer until reduced to sauce consistency, about 8 minutes. Stir in the basil and season to taste with salt and pepper.

4. Spoon the warm sauce over the chicken and pasta and serve.

TVP ANYONE?

Texturized vegetable protein—TVP—is a great way to stretch your meals. Made from soy flour cooked under pressure, extruded, and dried, TVP has a very long shelf life and contains up to 50% protein. These two qualities make it a fantastic addition to your pantry!

You can purchase TVP in "nuggets" that are somewhat equivalent in size to cubes of stewing beef, or in "crumbles" equivalent to ground beef. My personal preference is for the crumbles—when they are reconstituted and mixed in a 1:1 ratio with ground beef, even the most die-hard carnivore would be hard-pressed to distinguish between the two.

The mistake most first-timers make is to reconstitute their TVP with water alone. That will give you nothing but a bland, tasteless bowl of mush. Stirring it into cooked ground beef will improve things somewhat, but there's a much better way.

RECONSTITUTING TVP

To reconstitute TVP, simply add a boiling liquid. Use just slightly less liquid than TVP. For example, mix 7/8 cup of boiling liquid to 1 cup of TVP pieces. Cover with a lid and allow the granules or chunks to soak up the liquid. (Be sure to select a large enough bowl or pan, as TVP will approximately double in volume when reconstituted.) Stir the reconstituted TVP into the ground beef you're mixing it with.

The beauty of TVP is that it takes on the taste of whatever dish it's included in—so the key to a nicely flavored dish lies in the liquid you use to rehydrate your TVP. If you add seasonings to the water, the TVP will absorb them and be far more flavorful. These are some of my personal favorites:

- Onion soup mix
- Beef or chicken bouillon granules
- Chili powder and salt
- Garlic salt

Adding something with a bit of acidity will help flavor the protein and reconstitute it far more quickly. You only need a tablespoon or so of the acidic liquid ingredient per cup of TVP. A few possibilities are vinegar, ketchup, lemon juice, and tomato juice.

I find that TVP tastes best when used in a saucy, well-seasoned dish. It's virtually undetectable as anything other than ground beef when mixed into chili, spaghetti sauce, or taco filling. If you're following a recipe that calls for 1 pound of ground beef, you can use ½ pound of ground beef and ½ cup (before being reconstituted) of TVP.

Creamy Chicken Pasta

Serves 4

1 (4-ounce) package Knorr Pasta Sides of choice (such as Creamy Garlic Rafaello)

1 (12.5-ounce) can chunk chicken

1 (14-ounce) can creamed spinach or 1 (10.75-ounce) can creamed asparagus soup, drained well

grated Parmesan cheese, to taste

1. Prepare the pasta side dish according to the package directions.

2. Stir the chicken and spinach (or asparagus) into the hot pasta. Cover the pan tightly and let stand for 5 minutes. At this point it should be heated through; if not, turn on the burner to low and stir the mixture continuously until hot.

3. Top with Parmesan cheese and serve.

Spaghetti Casserole

Serves 4 to 5

1 pound spaghetti, cooked al dente and drained

1 (15-ounce) can spaghetti sauce

1 (14-ounce) can creamed spinach

1 (8-ounce) can sliced mushrooms, drained

½ cup fine breadcrumbs

¼ cup grated Parmesan cheese

2 tablespoons dried parsley

1. Preheat the oven to 400°F. Lightly grease a medium 1.8-liter casserole dish.

2. Mix the cooked spaghetti, spaghetti sauce, spinach, and mushrooms in the prepared casserole dish.

3. In a small bowl, stir together the breadcrumbs, Parmesan, and parsley. Sprinkle over the top of the casserole and bake for 30 minutes, or until heated through. If the top begins to get too brown, cover with foil.

Prepper's Beef Stroganoff

Serves 4 to 5

1 (1.6-ounce) packet mushroom gravy

3 cups egg noodles, cooked or 3 cups prepared rice

1 cup dried beef crumbles, rehydrated or 1 (12-ounce) can roast beef and gravy

1 cup dried peas, rehydrated

3 tablespoons dehydrated minced onions

1 teaspoon garlic powder

dash of nutmeg

salt and pepper

In a large skillet over medium-high heat, prepare the gravy according to the packet instructions. In the same skillet, combine all remaining ingredients and reduce heat to medium-low. Heat until the gravy begins to bubble. Serve hot.

Taco Pie

Serves 4 to 6

4 large flour or corn tortillas

1 (16-ounce) can refried beans

1 cup prepared mild salsa (page 67)

8 ounces Velveeta, cubed

1. Preheat the oven to 400°F.

2. In a greased pie pan, layer the ingredients 3 times in this order: tortilla, refried beans, ⅓ cup salsa, cheese. Top with the final tortilla and any remaining salsa and cheese.

3. Bake for 20 minutes, or until hot and bubbly.

4. Let stand for 10 minutes to thicken and then slice into wedges to serve.

Bandito's Casserole

Serves 4 to 6

1 pound ground beef (fresh or 1 cup dehydrated ground beef crumbles)

1 medium onion, chopped, or ⅓ cup dehydrated onion, rehydrated

1 (4.3-ounce) box Spanish rice

1 (15.4-ounce) can pinto beans, drained

2 cups water

1 tablespoon taco seasoning

1 teaspoon ground cumin

salt and pepper

1. In a skillet over medium-high heat, brown the beef or cook the rehydrated beef for 5 minutes. Add the onion and allow to cook for 2 to 3 minutes.

2. Add the remaining ingredients to the pan and allow the mixture to come to an active simmer. Cover and reduce the heat to low.

3. Cook for 15 minutes until the rice is tender and serve warm.

Baja Fish Tacos

Serves 6

BAJA SAUCE

¾ cup sour cream

juice of 1 lime

1 teaspoon chili powder

½ teaspoon ground cumin

1 teaspoon garlic powder

½ teaspoon onion powder

2 jalapeño chiles, finely chopped

TACOS

6 corn tortillas

1 to 2 pounds cod fish fillets, pan-fried

3 cups fresh shredded purple cabbage

1 bunch fresh cilantro, chopped

½ onion, thinly sliced

1. In a small bowl, stir together all the sauce ingredients until thoroughly blended.

2. In a skillet, warm the tortillas over medium heat for 30 seconds on each side. To assemble the tacos, fill each tortilla with a piece of fish, shredded cabbage, cilantro sprigs, and sliced onion.

3. With a spoon, add the Baja Sauce to the tacos.

Chicken and Rice

Serves 4 to 6

1 cup uncooked rice

2 tablespoons vegetable oil

½ onion, chopped or 3 tablespoons dehydrated chopped onion

1 garlic clove, minced

2 (12.5-ounce) cans chunk chicken, chopped

1 (6-ounce) can sliced mushrooms

3 cups water

1 tablespoon paprika

salt and pepper

1 to 2 tablespoons all-purpose flour

1. Cook the rice according to the package directions.

2. While the rice is cooking, heat the oil in a skillet over medium heat. Sauté the onion and garlic in the oil until soft. Add the

chicken and mushrooms and cook until everything begins to sizzle.

3. Pour the water into the skillet. Stir in the paprika and season to taste with salt and pepper. Cover and cook for 10 minutes, or until bubbly.

4. Spoon out 1 cup of the liquid into a bowl. Whisk in 1 tablespoon of flour, stirring until thickened. Add another tablespoon if not thick enough. Add back into the skillet and stir until the sauce has thickened.

5. Serve over the warm rice.

Chicken Jambalaya

Makes 4 to 5 servings

1 (12.5-ounce) can chunk chicken

1 cup uncooked white rice

½ cup stewed tomatoes

1 medium onion, chopped, or ⅓ cup dehydrated onion flakes

4 green onions, chopped, or 4 tablespoons dehydrated green onions

¼ cup chopped green bell peppers

⅓ cup chopped celery or 3 tablespoons dehydrated chopped celery

2 teaspoons Cajun seasoning, or more for extra heat

salt and pepper

¼ cup dry breadcrumbs

2 tablespoons butter, melted

1. Preheat the oven to 350°F. Lightly grease a 1.8-liter casserole dish.

2. In 4-quart a saucepan over medium heat, mix together the chicken, rice, and tomatoes. Allow to simmer, covered, for 10 minutes.

3. Add the onion, green onion, green pepper, and celery. Stir in the Cajun seasoning, salt, and pepper and stir well.

4. In a small bowl, combine the breadcrumbs and butter and stir until mixed thoroughly. Turn the jambalaya mixture into the baking dish and cover with the buttered crumbs. Bake for 1 hour.

King Chicken Casserole

Makes 8 servings

1 (10-ounce) can of Rotel tomatoes and chiles

1 (10-ounce) can condensed cream of mushroom soup

1 (10-ounce) can condensed cream of chicken soup

1 cup chopped yellow onion, fresh or ⅓ cup dehydrated yellow onion

2 (12.5-ounce) cans chunk chicken, drained

12 small corn tortillas, broken into pieces, or 4 cups crumbled tortilla chips

1 cup chicken broth

16 ounces Velveeta cheese, shredded and divided or 3 cups

dehydrated shredded sharp Cheddar cheese

1. Preheat the oven to 350°F. Lightly grease a 1.8-liter casserole dish.

2. In a large bowl, combine the tomatoes, soups, onion, and chicken.

3. In a medium bowl, soften the tortilla pieces or tortilla chips in the broth.

4. Layer the tortilla pieces, chicken mixture, and cheese in the baking dish. Repeat with remaining ingredients. Pour any remaining broth on top. Bake for 30 to 40 minutes.

Crispy Chicken Tostadas

Serves 4

4 (5-inch) flour tortillas

vegetable oil, for coating tortillas

1 (15.5-ounce) can refried beans

1 (12.5-ounce) can chicken breast

shredded cheddar cheese

1 (2.25-ounce) can black olives, drained, sliced

lettuce or sprouts

salsa, for serving

1. Preheat the oven to 375°F.

2. Brush the tortillas with oil on both sides. Place on a baking sheet and bake for 5 to 8 minutes, until golden brown.

Remove from the oven and let cool.

3. Top each tortilla with refried beans, chicken, cheese, and olives. Return to the oven for 5 minutes.

4. Top with lettuce or sprouts and serve with salsa.

Mexi-Tacos

For a crispier version, brush a light amount of oil on small corn tortillas, and bake them at 375°F for 8 minutes, flipping them over halfway through. *Serves 4*

1 tablespoon vegetable oil

½ onion, chopped

1 (15.4-ounce) can black beans, rinsed and drained

1 (15.4-ounce) can corn, rinsed and drained

¼ cup dehydrated red or green bell peppers, rehydrated

1 to 2 tablespoons coarsely chopped pickled jalapeños

1 tablespoon chili powder

¼ cup prepared salsa

salt and pepper

5 taco shells

1. Heat the oil in a skillet over medium heat. Sauté the onion in the oil until soft.

2. Stir in all the remaining ingredients except the taco shells and cook until heated through.

3. Spoon the hot filling into the taco shells and serve warm.

Mandarin Orange Chicken

Serves 4 to 5

1 tablespoon vegetable oil

2 (12.5-ounce) cans chunk chicken, drained

¾ cup mandarin oranges, undrained

¼ cup soy sauce

1 tablespoon cornstarch

¾ teaspoon prepared yellow mustard

1 tablespoon distilled white vinegar

¼ teaspoon garlic powder

1 tablespoon minced onions (fresh or dehydrated)

½ cup fresh green bell pepper, diced or ⅓ cup dehydrated diced bell peppers

cooked rice, for serving

1. Heat the oil in a skillet over medium heat. Sauté the chicken in the hot oil.

2. Meanwhile, whisk together the juice from the mandarin orange can with the soy sauce, cornstarch, yellow mustard, and vinegar in a small bowl; set aside.

3. In the skillet, add onions and bell peppers and stir. Add the marinade and pour over the chicken in the skillet.

4. Reduce heat to low and allow it to simmer. Add the oranges, cover with a lid, and cook 5 more minutes. Serve with rice.

Cola Canned Ham

Makes 10 servings

1 pound canned ham

1 (12-ounce) can cola

1. Preheat the oven to 300°F.

2. Do not remove the top of the ham can. Instead, use a "church key" can opener to puncture all around the top, spacing the holes about 2 inches apart. This will allow juices to drain from the ham later in the recipe.

3. Bake ham on a rimmed baking sheet in the oven for about 20 minutes to loosen the gelatin around the ham.

4. Remove from the oven and pour out the melted gelatin. Pour the cola in through the holes you've punched, using all of it.

5. Return the ham to the oven and cook for 1 hour.

6. Remove the ham from the oven, allow it to cool for a few minutes and then open. Remove ham from can and slice thinly to serve.

Slow-Cooker Tropical Ham

Serves 10

1 pound canned ham

1 (15-ounce) can crushed pineapple

1 cup orange juice

3 tablespoons light brown sugar

1 teaspoon ground allspice

1. Remove the ham from the can, draining the juices. Place the ham in a slow cooker.

2. In a medium bowl, mix the pineapple with the orange juice. Pour over the ham. Sprinkle the brown sugar on top.

3. Cover and cook on low for 8 hours.

Chipped Beef on Toast

This recipe—a Great Depression staple—can be adapted to whatever you have on hand. Instead of the beef, you can add bacon, ham, or Spam.

Serves 4 to 5

2 tablespoons butter

2 tablespoons all-purpose flour

1½ cups milk

2 cups dried beef crumbles or 1 (12-ounce) jar chipped beef

½ teaspoon garlic powder

½ teaspoon Worcestershire sauce

dash of cayenne pepper

salt and pepper

toast or cooked rice

1. In a 4-quart saucepan over medium heat, melt the butter. Whisk in the flour, stirring until a thick roux forms.

2. Reduce heat to low, and add the milk a little at a time, stirring continuously until the mixture thickens and comes to a steady simmer.

3. Stir in the beef and seasonings. Serve over toast or over rice.

Chili Mac

For a speedy version of this dish, simply stir a can of chili with beans into a prepared box of macaroni and cheese. *Serves 4 to 5*

1 pound ground beef

2 tablespoons chili powder

1 tablespoon onion powder

1 tablespoon garlic powder

1 (15-ounce) can pinto beans, rinsed and drained

1 (3-ounce) can tomato paste

2 cups uncooked elbow macaroni

1. In a skillet over medium-high heat, brown the ground beef, breaking it up as it browns. Once the beef is cooked through, drain it and add seasonings. Then, stir in the beans and tomato paste.

2. Meanwhile, cook the macaroni al dente according to the package directions.

3. Drain the cooked pasta and stir it into the ground beef mixture in the skillet. Heat through, stirring gently.

Beef and Potato Nachos

Serves 4 to 5

1 pound ground beef

1 (15-ounce) can kidney beans, rinsed and drained

1 tablespoon onion powder

1 (1-ounce) packet taco seasoning

1 (4.5-ounce) can tomato paste

½ cup water

3 cups cooked diced potatoes

1 (4.5-ounce) can diced green chiles

1 (10-ounce) can condensed Cheddar cheese soup

1 cup milk

½ teaspoon sugar

1. Preheat the oven to 350°F.

2. In a skillet, cook the ground beef thoroughly, breaking it up with a spoon, drain any residual grease.

3. Stir in the beans, onion powder, taco seasoning, tomato paste, and water. Spread this mixture in the bottom of a greased 1.8-liter casserole dish.

4. In a medium bowl, stir together the potatoes and chiles. Pour over the beef mixture in the pan.

5. Using the same bowl as for the potatoes, mix together the soup, milk, and sugar. Pour evenly over the casserole in the pan.

6. Bake, covered, for 1 hour. Uncover and bake another 15 minutes. Let stand for 10 minutes before serving.

Macaroni and Tomatoes

Serves 4 to 6

1 (8-ounce) package elbow macaroni

2 tablespoons butter, divided

1 small onion, chopped or ⅓ cup dehydrated chopped onions, rehydrated

1 (14.5-ounce) can tomato paste or 1 cup ketchup (purchased or made from recipe on page 54)

½ teaspoon granulated sugar

1 (14-ounce) can diced tomatoes

salt and pepper

1. Cook the macaroni according to the package directions until al dente. Drain and add to a bowl with 1 tablespoon of butter. Stir pasta to melt the butter, set aside.

2. In a skillet over medium heat, melt the remaining butter and sauté the onion until tender. Stir in the tomato paste (or ketchup) and sugar and let simmer for 5 minutes.

3. Add the tomatoes and then the cooked macaroni. Season with salt and pepper to taste.

4. Stir and simmer, uncovered, over low heat for 15 minutes.

Pasta e Fagioli

Serves 4 to 5

1 tablespoon olive oil

2 tablespoons dried minced onion

2 tablespoons dried minced garlic

¼ cup dehydrated or freeze-dried carrots

1 tablespoon dried basil

2 teaspoons dried oregano

dash of red pepper flakes

1 (14.5-ounce) can diced tomatoes, with juices

3 cups low-sodium chicken broth or vegetable broth, or 3 bouillon cubes mixed with 3 cups water, plus more as needed

1 (15.8-ounce) can Great Northern beans, rinsed and drained

HOT SPAM!

Name one processed food more iconic than the humble SPAM. I dare you.

What other "Specially Processed Assorted Meat" has its own museum in Austin, Minnesota, a Broadway musical named after it (Monty Python's Spamalot), and even an annual festival (Spamarama, in Austin, Texas)?

SPAM was created by Hormel in 1926 and marketed as Hormel Spiced Ham, the Miracle Meat in a Can. A 1937 contest to find a new name yielded the moniker SPAM—SPiced hAM. (Over the years, the acronym has represented Shoulder Pork and hAM, and then Specially Processed Assorted Meats.) SPAM came into its own during WWII, when meat rations were in effect.

SHOULD SPAM GO IN YOUR PREPPER PANTRY?

The Miracle Meat in a Can has a reputation for being less than appetizing, but enough cans were sold before the year 2000 to wrap around the world almost 10½ times. The average resident of Hawaii—the state with the highest Spam sales per capita—consumes more than four cans a year.

Spam is actually ready to eat right from the can. However, many feel the texture is improved when Spam is cooked. Consider these ways to use it:

- Thinly sliced and sautéed, as a sandwich filling or in place of ham or bacon for breakfast
- Diced and fried with potatoes and vegetables
- Diced and mixed into casseroles or pasta dishes
- Browned for Southern Biscuits and Gravy (page 91)
- Diced as a filling for tacos or fajitas
- Diced and included in potato salad or macaroni salad

Though a single serving of the product contains 16 grams of fat and more than half the RDA of sodium, in moderation Spam isn't going to kill you. Anyone with good cholesterol levels and reasonable blood pressure should be able to eat it from time to time with no ill effects.

---

1 cup uncooked tiny pasta shells (ditalini)

2 tablespoons parsley

grated Parmesan cheese and freshly ground black pepper, for topping

1. In a large, heavy pot over medium heat, combine the olive oil, onion, garlic, and carrots. Cook for 3 minutes, stirring, until carrots soften, about 5 minutes.

2. Add the dried basil, oregano, and red pepper flakes and toss to coat with the oil. Stir in the tomatoes and broth; bring to a boil.

3. Reduce the heat low and simmer, uncovered, for 30 minutes.

4. If the sauce seems too thick, add 1 cup of stock or water to thin, then stir in the beans and pasta. Simmer for 6 to 8 minutes, or until the pasta is tender. Stir in the parsley.

5. Serve hot, topped with grated Parmesan and freshly ground black pepper.

Golden Noodles with Browned Butter

Makes 4 to 6 servings

2 tablespoons butter

3 cups egg noodles, cooked

2 tablespoons powdered Parmesan cheese

2 teaspoons dehydrated minced parsley

salt

1. In a small saucepan over medium heat, melt the butter until it darkens in color. Remove from the heat.

2. In a large bowl, toss the cooked noodles with the butter sauce. Add salt to taste and sprinkle the noodles with Parmesan cheese and parsley. Serve hot.

Spaghetti Salad

Makes 6 servings

8 ounces uncooked spaghetti

2 teaspoons seasoning salt

3 tablespoons lemon juice

¼ cup Italian dressing

1 tomato, diced or ⅓ cup dehydrated diced tomato

1 cup diced fresh green bell pepper or ¼ cup dehydrated diced celery, rehydrated

½ cup chopped fresh celery or ¼ cup dehydrated chopped celery, rehydrated

½ cup diced onion, fresh or 4 tablespoons dehydrated chopped onion, rehydrated

1 (3.25-ounce) can sliced black olives, drained

¼ teaspoon ground black pepper

2 teaspoons grated Parmesan cheese

1. Cook the spaghetti according to the package directions. Drain.

2. In a large bowl, mix the cooked spaghetti and remaining ingredients and stir to combine. Serve chilled or at room temperature.

Mac and Cheese

Makes 5 servings

1 (8-ounce) package elbow macaroni

4 tablespoons butter, divided

3 tablespoons all-purpose flour

1 garlic clove

2 cups milk

2 cups shredded Cheddar cheese or 2 cups dehydrated shredded sharp cheddar cheese

1 teaspoon dry mustard

1 cup dry breadcrumbs

salt and pepper

2½ ounces bacon bits (optional)

1. Cook the macaroni according to the package directions. Meanwhile, preheat the oven to 425°F.

2. Drain the pasta and add to a lightly greased, 2.8-liter casserole dish along with 2 tablespoons of the butter. Stir until butter has melted.

3. Melt the remaining 2 tablespoons butter in a saucepan over low heat and slowly whisk in the flour. Cook, stirring, for 3 minutes until the mixture looks paste-like.

4. Add the garlic clove and slowly stir in the milk, whisking continuously until the sauce comes to a boil. Stir and cook an additional 5 minutes to let the sauce thicken.

5. Stir in the cheese, dry mustard, and season to taste with salt and pepper. Remove the garlic clove.

6. Pour the sauce over the cooked macaroni in the casserole dish. Top with the breadcrumbs.

7. Bake for 15 minutes, until the breadcrumbs are lightly toasted and the casserole is heated through.

Potato Gnocchi

6 fist-sized russet white potatoes

2 cups all-purpose flour

½ cup olive oil

1 egg

¼ teaspoon salt

marinara sauce or pesto, to serve

1. Boil the potatoes in their skins until soft. Once cooled, remove the skins.

2. Mash with a fork, or purée in the blender or food mill until the texture is similar to creamy mashed potatoes.

3. Bring a medium pot of water to a boil. On the counter next to the stove, prepare an ice bath with 6 cups ice and 6 cups water (or just use cold water).

4. In a large mixing bowl, combine the potatoes, flour, oil, egg, and salt, mixing well to create a dough. Knead the dough for 4 to 5 minutes, or until it feels dry to the touch.

5. Roll out the dough to ¾ inch thick, then cut it into strips with a pizza cutter or a knife.

6. Pick up the strips with a fork and drop them into the boiling water for 1 minute; when they are done they will float to the top of the water.

7. Immediately remove the cooked gnocchi and place it in the ice bath until cooled.

8. Drain the gnocchi well and serve with marinara sauce or pesto sauce.

7 BEANS AND RICE

Beans and rice are the best pantry budget stretchers, bar none. Forming a complete protein when served together, they can serve twenty people for less than $5! Their tremendous amount of fiber is filling, and adding some tasty seasonings can make these humble ingredients into a delicious, satisfying meal.

BEANS, BEANS, THE MAGICAL FRUIT

Most bean eaters today open a can and dump it out. But beans purchased in cans are far less tasty and a lot pricier than beans cooked from scratch. Canned beans are a great pantry addition for those times when cooking facilities are limited or when time is a factor, but you can't beat home-cooked beans for taste and economy.

STEP 1: Rinse and sort. Dried beans are often dirty, and you might even find the occasional insect. Not to worry— the first step gets rid of all that. Take a handful at a time, scanning for dried or withered legumes. Put them in a pot and cover with water. Swish them around and then drain them in a colander. Rinse briefly under running water.

STEP 2: Soak. Most beans cook far more quickly if they've been soaked first for 8 hours or more. (Split peas, lentils, black-eyed peas, chickpeas, black beans, lima beans, and fava beans don't require soaking.) To soak, cover the beans with water by about 2 inches and let them soak for 8 hours or longer. The beans will expand a great deal, so make sure to use a big enough container.

Soaking beans has another significant benefit—it loosens the outer skin and removes the oligosaccharides, the indigestible complex sugars that can cause intestinal gas.

Quick-soak method—If you forget to start soaking your beans far enough ahead of time, you can use this method to speed things up. Place the rinsed and sorted beans in a pot, cover them with water by about 2 inches, and bring to a boil. Cover the pot, remove from the heat, and let the beans soak. This can reduce your soaking time to 2 to 3 hours.

STEP 3: Cook. After soaking your beans, dump out the soaking water (plants love this water!) and rinse the beans. Place in a large stockpot and cover with 3 to 4 times as much water as beans. Bring to a boil, then reduce to a simmer. Note: Kidney, cannellini, and butter beans must be boiled on high for 10 minutes to neutralize a toxin that can cause extreme intestinal distress.

Expect to cook beans for 1 to 1½ hours, until they are tender and slightly soft. Split peas only take 30 to 45 minutes. All legumes and beans should be cooked thoroughly for ease of digestion.

RICE 101

Rice is the primary food staple of more than three billion people worldwide. It is inexpensive, versatile, and nutritious. Rice contains eight essential amino acids and fifteen vitamins and minerals, and it's a great source of complex carbohydrates.

A single grain of rice is made up of several layers. The outer layer is an inedible hull. Only this hull is removed in the processing of brown rice, leaving the other nutritious layers intact. Sometimes brown rice is milled further, removing the bran and the germ, leaving it less nutritious. This is when brown rice starts getting stripped of its nutritional content. For white rice, the processing is taken a step further and the grain is polished, removing most of the nutritional value.

The downside to brown rice is that because it contains the oil-rich wheat germ, it's less stable. Brown rice can become rancid in as little as six months. That's why white rice, though far less nutritious, still has a place of value in a food storage pantry.

COOKING TECHNIQUES

The easiest way to cook rice is to bake it. It's absolutely foolproof. In a grid-down situation, if your oven is gas, you may still be able to use this method.

2 cups rice

4 cups water or stock

seasonings of choice

FOR BROWN RICE:

1. Preheat the oven to 375°F.

2. Put the rice and water or stock in a 4-quart saucepan and bring to a boil on the stovetop over medium-high heat.

3. Cover tightly with a lid and immediately place the pan in the oven.

4. Cook for exactly 1 hour—no peeking. Perfect fluffy rice!

FOR WHITE RICE:

1. Preheat the oven to 350°F.

2. Put the rice and water in a saucepan and bring to a boil on the stovetop over medium-high heat.

3. Cover tightly with an ovenproof lid and immediately place the pan in the oven.

4. Cook for exactly 30 minutes—no peeking. Perfect fluffy rice!

20 WAYS TO EAT BEANS AND RICE

A simple pot of cooked beans and rice can offer amazing variety with nothing more than a change of herbs, spices, and other additions. Prepare your beans and rice as directed, season them abundantly—and don't be afraid to adjust the seasonings to suit your family's preferences.

Most of the following recipes don't include step-by-step instructions. They are really just ways to jazz up your already-cooked beans and rice. Simply combine all the ingredients in a 6-quart saucepan and simmer over medium heat for about 10 minutes.

Arroz con Frijole

Serves 5 to 6

4 cups prepared white or brown rice

1 (15-ounce) can pinto beans, undrained and rinsed

1 tablespoon chili powder

2 teaspoons ground cumin

1 teaspoon garlic powder

1 teaspoon onion powder

1 tablespoon beef bouillon granules

1 (3-ounce) can tomato paste

Rice Fagioli

Serves 5

4 cups prepared white or brown rice

1 (15-ounce) can cannellini beans (white kidney beans), undrained

1 tablespoon garlic powder

1 tablespoon chicken bouillon granules

2 cups fresh spinach leaves

2 teaspoons Italian seasoning

grated Parmesan cheese, for serving

salt and pepper

Baltimore Beans and Rice

Serves 5 to 6

4 cups prepared white or brown rice

3 to 4 cups cooked black-eyed peas

1 cup fresh kale or spinach, chopped

1 tablespoon apple cider vinegar

1 tablespoon Worcestershire sauce

1 (15-ounce) can whole kernel corn, rinsed and drained

2 tablespoons Old Bay or Chesapeake seafood seasoning

Asian Beans and Rice

Serves 5 to 6

4 cups prepared white or brown rice

3 to 4 cups cooked black beans or adzuki beans

1 cup cooked diced carrots

¼ cup diced green onions or freeze-dried chives

1 teaspoon ground ginger

2 tablespoons soy sauce

1 (11-ounce) can mandarin oranges with juice

1 teaspoon Chinese five-spice powder

Mediterranean Beans and Rice

Serves 5 to 6

- 4 cups prepared white or brown rice
- 3 to 4 cups cooked cannellini beans (white kidney beans)
- 1 (6-ounce) jar marinated artichoke hearts, drained and chopped
- 1 teaspoon celery seed powder
- 1 tablespoon garlic powder
- ½ cup whole pitted green olives
- 1 tablespoon lemon juice
- 1 tablespoon dried parsley
- 1 teaspoon dried dill weed
- salt and pepper

Indian Beans and Rice

Serves 5 to 6

- 4 cups prepared white or brown rice
- 3 to 4 cups cooked chickpeas
- 1 tablespoon curry powder
- ½ teaspoon ground cinnamon
- 1 cup canned diced tomatoes with green chiles
- 1 teaspoon ground ginger
- salt and pepper
- 1 tablespoon chopped fresh cilantro (if available)

Lentil Stew with Rice

Serves 5 to 6

- 4 cups prepared white or brown rice
- 3 to 4 cups cooked brown lentils
- 1 teaspoon onion powder
- 1 teaspoon garlic powder
- 1 (15-ounce) can diced or stewed tomatoes
- 1 tablespoon dried thyme

East Indian Lentils and Rice

Serves 5 to 6

- 4 cups prepared white or brown rice
- 3 to 4 cups cooked brown lentils
- 1 cup cooked diced carrots
- 1 tablespoon minced garlic
- 1 teaspoon ground coriander
- 1 teaspoon ground cumin
- salt and pepper

Dal with Rice

Serves 5 to 6

- 4 cups prepared white or brown rice
- 3 to 4 cups cooked red lentils
- 1 teaspoon ground coriander
- 1 teaspoon ground cumin
- 1 tablespoon garlic powder
- 1 teaspoon curry powder
- 2 tablespoons lemon juice
- salt and pepper

New Orleans Red Beans and Rice

Serves 5 to 6

- 4 cups prepared white or brown rice
- 3 to 4 cups cooked red kidney beans
- 1 tablespoon dehydrated onion flakes
- 1 tablespoon dried minced garlic
- 1 tablespoon dehydrated bell pepper
- 1 cup diced ham
- 1 teaspoon cayenne pepper
- 1 teaspoon dried thyme
- 1 teaspoon dried sage
- 1 teaspoon dried parsley
- 1 tablespoon Cajun seasoning

Creole Hoppin' John

Serves 5 to 6

- 4 cups prepared white or brown rice
- 3 to 4 cups cooked black-eyed peas
- 1 tablespoon onion powder
- 1 teaspoon garlic powder
- 1 teaspoon paprika
- 1 tablespoon chili powder
- ½ teaspoon cayenne pepper
- 1 teaspoon dried thyme
- 1 cup diced fresh tomatoes

New Year's Day Hoppin' John

Serves 5 to 6

- 4 cups prepared white or brown rice
- 3 to 4 cups cooked black-eyed peas
- 1 cup diced ham or meat from 1 leftover ham bone
- salt and pepper
- 1 teaspoon garlic powder
- 1 tablespoon onion powder
- crushed red pepper flakes, to taste

Cuban Beans and Rice

Serves 5 to 6

4 cups prepared white or brown rice

3 to 4 cups cooked black beans

1 tablespoon dried bell peppers (or 1 tablespoon fresh, if available)

1 tablespoon chili powder

1 teaspoon garlic powder

1 teaspoon onion powder

1 tablespoon lemon or lime juice

1 tablespoon fresh cilantro (if available), chopped

Cuban Beans and Rice II

Serves 5 to 6

4 cups prepared white or brown rice

3 to 4 cups cooked black beans

1 (15-ounce) can Rotel tomatoes with chiles

1 (15-ounce) can whole kernel corn, rinsed and drained

1 tablespoon chili powder

1 tablespoon garlic powder

1 teaspoon onion powder

1 tablespoon lemon or lime juice

1 tablespoon chopped fresh cilantro (if available)

Louisiana Country Beans and Rice

Serves 5 to 6

4 cups prepared white or brown rice

3 to 4 cups cooked red kidney beans

1 (15-ounce) can Rotel tomatoes with green chiles

1 tablespoon dehydrated onion flakes

1 tablespoon dried minced garlic

1 tablespoon dried oregano

dash of hot sauce, or to taste

Lemon Black Beans and Rice

Serves 5 to 6

4 cups prepared white or brown rice

3 to 4 cups cooked black beans

1 tablespoon lemon juice

1 teaspoon garlic powder

1 tablespoon chopped fresh cilantro (if available)

Pirate Beans and Rice

Serves 5 to 6

4 cups prepared white or brown rice

3 to 4 cups cooked black beans

1 tablespoon dark rum

2 tablespoons dark brown sugar

½ cup diced carrots, cooked

1 tablespoon garlic powder

1 tablespoon onion powder

1 tablespoon dried parsley

salt and pepper

Beefy Enchilada Beans and Rice

Serves 5 to 6

4 cups prepared white or brown rice

3 to 4 cups cooked pinto beans

1 pound ground beef, cooked, or 1 cup dehydrated meat crumbles

½ cup canned diced green chiles

1 (10-ounce) can tomato paste

1 tablespoon chili powder

1 teaspoon ground cumin

1 tablespoon garlic powder

1 teaspoon onion powder

Bean Fried Rice

Serves 5 to 6

4 cups prepared white or brown rice

3 to 4 cups cooked black beans

1 teaspoon ground ginger

1 teaspoon Chinese five-spice powder

¼ cup chopped green onions or chives

1 cup canned peas and carrots, drained

1 tablespoon soy sauce

1 tablespoon plum sauce

Haitian Beans and Rice

Serves 5 to 6

4 cups prepared white or brown rice

3 to 4 cups cooked red kidney beans

1 tablespoon onion powder

1 tablespoon garlic powder

2 bay leaves

¼ teaspoon ground cloves

2 tablespoons dried parsley

Southwest Sweet Potatoes

Serves 5 to 6

1 cup peeled and cubed sweet
potato or yams

2 tablespoons vegetable oil

½ cup sliced onions

½ cup sliced green peppers,
julienned

1 cup fresh or canned whole corn
kernels

1 tablespoon ground cumin

dash of cayenne pepper

salt and pepper

4 cups prepared white or brown rice

2 cups cooked black beans

1 avocado, diced (optional)

shredded Cheddar cheese (optional)

1 Preheat oven to 350°F. On a lightly greased baking sheet, bake the sweet potatoes or yams until soft, 25 to 30 minutes.

2. Meanwhile, heat the oil in a large skillet over medium heat until it begins to sizzle. Sauté the onions, peppers, and corn in the hot oil until they reach the desired doneness. Season with cumin, cayenne, salt, and pepper. Add beans and allow mixture to simmer. When the sweet potatoes or yams are cooked, add them to the mixture and let simmer for 10 minutes before serving.

3. To serve, top with cheese and avocado, if using.

KID-APPROVED SNACKS

Caring for kids in the midst of a crisis can be difficult. Children have a psychological need for security and stability, and when they are in a chaotic and unpredictable environment, they pick up on the stress and may act out, regress, or withdraw.

Including your children in preparations can help them learn to adapt to the situation at hand. One woman shared that when her family was in the middle of an emergency, they sat together and said, "We're not scared, because we're prepared." Repeating this simple sentence helped her family find a sense of peace, knowing that Mom and Dad had the situation handled and were ready for whatever might happen.

Let your kids feel like part of the solution by allowing them to ask questions and give their input. Enlist their assistance—most kids love helping out Mom or Dad! Adding some of their favorite foods to the emergency menu will help give them a sense of normality. You want to help your child realize that this is only a minor inconvenience, and that things will be all right. This can be a powerful tool in a parent's arsenal.

Applesauce

Serves 4

- 6 sweet apples (such as Gala, Jonathan, or McIntosh), peeled, cored, and quartered
- 1 teaspoon ground cinnamon (optional)
- ¾ cup water
- 3 tablespoons brown sugar (optional)

1. Place the apples in a medium saucepan over medium-low heat. Sprinkle with cinnamon, if you wish. Add the water and cook, covered, until the apple bits become soft, about 10 minutes.

2. Using a blender or a potato masher, mash the apples until the sauce has the texture you want.

3. Stir in brown sugar, if desired, and mix well.

Graham Crackers

Makes 4 dozen

- ½ cup vegetable shortening
- ¾ cup packed light brown sugar
- 1½ teaspoons vanilla extract
- 1½ cups whole wheat flour
- ½ cup all-purpose flour
- 1 teaspoon baking powder
- ½ teaspoon baking soda
- ¼ teaspoon salt
- 1 teaspoon ground cinnamon
- ½ cup milk
- ½ cup ground flax seed or wheat germ, or 2 tablespoons honey (optional)

1. In a medium bowl, cream together the shortening and brown sugar with a spoon. Stir in the vanilla.

2. In a large bowl, combine the whole-wheat and all-purpose flours, baking powder, baking soda, salt, and cinnamon. Beat into the creamed mixture alternately with the milk. Stir in the flax seed, wheat germ, or honey, if using. Cover and chill until firm.

3. Preheat the oven to 350°F. Grease two baking sheets.

4. On a lightly floured surface, roll the dough to a ⅛-inch thickness. Cut into 2-inch rectangles for mini graham crackers or cut into 4-inch rectangles for traditional-size crackers. Place ½ inch apart on the prepared cookie sheets.

5. Bake for 10 to 12 minutes in the preheated oven, until crisp. The edges will be golden brown. Remove from baking sheet to cool on wire racks. Store in an airtight container for up to 2 weeks.

Oatmeal Snack Mix

Serves 3 to 4

2 cups rolled oats

½ cup honey

1 teaspoon ground cinnamon

1 teaspoon salt

1 cup dried apple cubes or other dried fruit (or a combination)

½ cup nuts (whatever you have on hand, such as pecans, walnuts, or almonds)

2 cups square cereal pieces (oat, corn, or rice)

1. Preheat the oven to 325°F.

2. Lightly spray a rimmed baking sheet with cooking spray. Spread the oatmeal on the sheet and drizzle with the honey. Sprinkle with the cinnamon and salt.

3. Bake for 20 minutes, removing from the oven every 5 minutes to stir.

4. Stir in the fruit, nuts, and cereal squares. Let cool and then store in an airtight container.

Homemade Saltine Crackers

Makes 30 crackers

2 cups all-purpose flour

¾ teaspoon salt, plus more for sprinkling

⅔ cup milk

3 tablespoons butter, melted, plus more for brushing

½ teaspoon baking soda

10 ounces shredded Cheddar cheese or 1 (1-ounce) packet ranch dressing mix (optional)

1. Preheat the oven to 400°F. Grease a baking sheet.

2. In a large bowl, stir together the flour, ¾ teaspoon salt, milk, butter, and baking soda. If you want to make flavored crackers, stir in cheese or ranch dressing mix. Knead the dough well for 1 or 2 minutes.

3. On a floured surface, roll the dough very thin, about ⅛ inch thick. Transfer in one piece to the baking sheet.

4. Score the dough with a pizza cutter or knife. Brush the top very lightly with butter and sprinkle with a little salt. (You can leave out this step if you want unsalted crackers.)

5. Bake for about 12 minutes. Let crackers cool on a wire rack. They will harden once they start to cool. Break into pieces and store in an airtight container.

Chunky Peanut Butter Balls

To add a special touch, roll the balls in crushed graham crackers or cookies before chilling them. *Makes 20 balls*

1 cup chunky peanut butter

1 cup quick-cooking rolled oats, toasted in the oven

⅓ cup crushed dehydrated apples

¾ teaspoon vanilla extract

½ teaspoon ground cinnamon

dash of salt

1 bar dark chocolate, melted, for drizzling (optional)

1. Combine all ingredients except the melted chocolate, if using, in a medium bowl and stir well to combine.

2. Spoon out a heaping tablespoon of the mixture and roll between your hands to form a ball. Place on a plate. Repeat to make the rest of the peanut butter balls.

3. Cover and refrigerate for a couple of hours. If using the melted chocolate, drizzle the chocolate on the chilled peanut butter balls before serving. Chill for an additional 20 minutes for chocolate to set.

Chocolate Crackers

Makes 20 crackers

about 20 saltine crackers, either store-bought or Homemade Saltine Crackers (page 148)

¾ cup unsalted butter

¾ cup packed brown sugar

¼ teaspoon vanilla extract

4 cups semisweet chocolate chips

½ cup toffee bits, peanut butter chips, cookie sprinkles, or other topping (optional)

1. Preheat the oven to 375°F.

2. Line a rimmed baking sheet with foil and arrange the crackers on the foil so they aren't touching.

3. In a 1-quart saucepan over low heat, stir together the butter, brown sugar, and vanilla until the butter is melted and the sugar is well incorporated. Pour the mixture over the crackers and place in the oven for 5 minutes.

5. Remove from the oven and sprinkle the chocolate chips onto the crackers. As the chocolate begins to melt, spread it over the cracker tops until they are evenly coated. If you wish, sprinkle on toffee bits, peanut butter chips, or your favorite topping.

7. Place the partly cooled baking sheet in the refrigerator to chill completely. Store in an airtight container.

Yummus Hummus

Accompany this dip alongside raw veggies, pita chips, or crackers. It can also be used as a sandwich spread. *Serves 2 to 3*

1 (15-ounce) can chickpeas, rinsed and drained

2 tablespoons lemon juice

¼ cup extra-virgin olive oil, plus more for drizzling

2 garlic cloves, crushed and minced

½ teaspoon sea salt

1½ teaspoons ground cumin

⅛ teaspoon cayenne pepper

chopped parsley, for garnish

Place the chickpeas, lemon juice, ¼ cup olive oil, garlic, salt, cumin, and cayenne in the bowl of a food processor. Process until smooth. To serve, drizzle with more olive oil and garnish with parsley.

Carrot-Orange Salad

Serves 4 to 5

5 to 7 carrots, peeled

2 apples, peeled and cored

juice of 1 orange or other citrus fruit

chopped pineapple (optional)

1. Shred the carrots and apples in a food processor or with a cheese grater. (If you have a food processor, it will save you time and energy!)

2. Transfer the shredded carrots and apples to a large bowl and squeeze orange juice over them.

3. Cover and refrigerate for 1 hour to allow the flavors to meld. Serve chilled.

Good Ol' Bean Dip

Offer homemade tortilla chips or crisp vegetables for dipping. To make a spicier dip, add a dash of cayenne pepper. *Serves 2 to 3*

1 (15-ounce) can refried beans

1 tablespoon brine from bottled jalapeño slices

½ teaspoon ground cumin

½ teaspoon salt

½ teaspoon white pepper

½ teaspoon granulated sugar

1 teaspoon chili powder

Mix all the ingredients together in a bowl until thoroughly blended. Cover and chill for at least 1 hour before serving.

Cowboy Crackers

Makes about 25 crackers

1 sleeve of packaged saltine crackers or 38 Homemade Saltine Crackers (page 148)

1 (.4-ounce) packet ranch dressing mix

1⅓ cups vegetable oil

⅛ to ¼ teaspoon crushed red pepper flakes

1. Preheat oven to 250°F. Place the crackers in a 1-gallon zip-top plastic bag.

2. Whisk together the remaining ingredients in a small bowl. Pour the mixture over the crackers and shake to coat.

3. Lay the bag flat and flip it over every 10 minutes for 1 hour to make sure all the crackers are generously coated.

4. Place spiced crackers on a baking sheet and bake for 20 minutes.

Cinnamon Apple Protein Snack

Serves 3 to 4

1 tablespoon ground cinnamon

1 (1-ounce) scoop vanilla protein powder

3 large apples, peeled, cored, and sliced

Pour the cinnamon and protein powder into a resealable plastic bag. Add the apples, seal the bag, and shake until the slices are coated with the cinnamon mixture. Serve immediately.

Granola

Serves 8

3 cups rolled oats

½ cup sweetened flaked coconut

½ cup coarsely chopped nuts (such almonds, pecans, or peanuts)

½ cup unsalted shelled sunflower seeds

½ cup honey or maple syrup

⅓ cup vegetable oil

¼ teaspoon ground cinnamon

dash of almond extract

dash of coconut extract

½ to 1 cup dried fruit (cherries, apples, bananas, cranberries, raisins, or blueberries are great choices)

¼ cup semisweet chocolate chips (optional)

1. Preheat the oven to 300°F.

2. Combine all the ingredients in a large bowl and stir thoroughly. Spread on a rimmed baking sheet.

3. Bake for 20 to 25 minutes, or until lightly toasted. The granola will crisp up more as it cools. Allow to cool completely, then store in an airtight container.

PB and Jelly Oat Bars

Serves 8 to 10

1 cup firmly packed dark brown sugar

¾ cup unsalted butter or vegetable shortening

½ cup peanut butter

2 cups all-purpose flour

1 teaspoon salt

½ teaspoon baking soda

1½ cups instant rolled oats

½ cup unsalted shelled sunflower seeds

dash of vanilla extract

⅓ cup water

1 cup jelly (your choice of flavor)

1. Preheat the oven to 400°F. Grease a 13 x 9-inch baking pan.

2. In the bowl of an electric mixer, combine the brown sugar, butter or shortening, and peanut butter. Beat on medium speed until well blended.

3. In a medium bowl, stir together the flour, salt, and baking soda.

At low speed, gradually add the dry ingredients to the creamed mixture. Stir in the oats, sunflower seeds, and vanilla until well blended. With the mixer running, add the water 1 tablespoon at a time.

4. Divide the dough in half and press half of it into the bottom of the greased pan. Spread evenly with the jelly.

5. Flatten small amounts of the remaining dough between your hands and arrange evenly on top of the jelly so that the dough sections are touching. Fill in any spaces with dough so that the jelly is completely covered.

6. Bake for 25 to 30 minutes, or until the top is golden brown and the edges are slightly brown. Do not overbake.

7. While warm, cut into bars about 2½ by 2 inches. Allow to cool completely and store in an airtight container.

Cheese Crackers

Add extra seasonings for different cracker flavors. Red pepper flakes, taco seasoning, or ranch dressing mix will add flair to this recipe.

Makes about 75 crackers

- ¼ cup (½ stick) butter, at room temperature
- 1¾ cups shredded Cheddar cheese
- ½ teaspoon sea salt, plus a bit more to sprinkle on top
- ¾ cup all-purpose flour, plus more for dusting
- 2 tablespoons milk

1. In a large bowl, cream the butter, cheese, and salt together until completely blended. Add the flour and mix until the dough is soft and crumbly. Add 1 tablespoon of milk at a time until the dough comes together.

2. Refrigerate the dough, covered, for 1 hour.

3. Preheat the oven to 350°F.

4. On a floured surface, roll the chilled dough to a thickness of about ⅛ inch. Divide in half. On a piece of parchment paper, roll half of the dough into a very thin 12 x 9-inch rectangle. Cut into 1-inch squares, using a pizza cutter; arrange on parchment paper and lift the sheet of parchment onto a baking sheet. Repeat with the other half of the dough.

5. Using a fork or toothpick, poke holes in the center of each cracker and sprinkle with salt.

6. Bake for 10 for 15 minutes, or until the crackers are puffed up and beginning to brown on the edges. Transfer the crackers to a wire rack or plate to cool. When completely cool, store in an airtight container.

9 SIDE DISHES

Incorporating vegetables into a meal to go along with the main dish is a great opportunity to add vitamins and other nutrients and provide a more complete meal for your family. Many of the following dishes can be refined to suit your individual preference or situation. Keep in mind that many can be adapted using freeze-dried or dehydrated ingredients to provide nutrition not only in the summertime, but all year—see to the chart on page 116.

Sautéed Spinach

Serves 4 to 5

1 tablespoon olive oil

2 garlic cloves, sliced

5 cups spinach, washed and chopped

salt and pepper

Heat the oil in a skillet over medium heat. Sauté the sliced garlic in the oil for 1 minute. Add the spinach and cook for 1 minute. Serve warm.

Sautéed Cabbage and Bacon

Serves 6

3 bacon slices, cooked and chopped, or ¼ cup bacon bits

½ onion, chopped

1 head cabbage, chopped

salt and pepper

1. In a large pan, heat the bacon pieces over medium heat to release the bacon grease. Add the onion and sauté with the bacon for 2 minutes.

2. Add the cabbage and sauté, stirring, for 4 minutes.

3. Season with salt and pepper to taste.

Spiced Vegetable Medley

This makes a great vegetarian taco filling. Add a cup of beans, and you're set! For a spicier version, chop and sauté a jalapeño chile in with vegetables. *Serves 4 to 5*

1 tablespoon olive oil

½ onion, chopped

3 garlic cloves, minced

kernels from 2 ears of corn

1 zucchini, diced

1 yellow squash, diced

1 bell pepper, chopped

2 tablespoons chili powder

salt and pepper

1 cup spinach, chopped

1. Heat the olive oil in a large skillet over medium heat. Sauté the onion in the oil for 2 minutes. Add the garlic and sauté for an additional minute.

2. Add the corn, zucchini, summer squash, and bell pepper. Cook for 4 minutes, stirring frequently, or until the vegetables begin to soften.

3. Season with the chili powder, salt, and pepper, stirring well.

4. Turn off heat and stir in the spinach. Serve warm.

Peas with Lemon Pepper

Serves 4

1 (10-ounce) package frozen peas, thawed, or 1 (15-ounce) can peas

1 tablespoon water

2 tablespoons butter

2 teaspoons lemon pepper seasoning

⅛ teaspoon dried dill

salt and pepper

Combine all the ingredients in a 4-quart saucepan over medium heat. Heat, stirring, until the mixture reaches an active simmer.

Stewed Lentils

Serves 4 to 6

1 cup lentils

2½ cups water

2 teaspoons olive oil

1 cup dehydrated carrots

1 tablespoon minced dried garlic

1 tablespoon minced dried onion

1 (28-ounce) can diced tomatoes

2 vegetable or beef bouillon cubes

2 teaspoons mild curry powder

2 teaspoons dried thyme

1 tablespoon red wine vinegar

salt and pepper

1. Rinse and pick over the lentils to remove any stones or debris.

2. Place the lentils in a 4-quart saucepan and pour in the water. Add the olive oil, carrots, garlic, onion, tomatoes, bouillon, curry, and thyme.

3. Bring to a boil over medium-high heat, then lower the heat to medium-low and simmer, covered, for about 40 minutes, or until the lentils are tender. Check occasionally to be sure the liquid is still simmering; add more water if needed.

4. Remove from the heat and allow the lentils to sit, covered, for another 10 minutes. Stir in the vinegar, season to taste with salt and pepper, and serve hot.

Creamed Peas

Serves 4

1 (10-ounce) package frozen peas, thawed, or 1 (15-ounce) can peas

1 tablespoon butter

⅓ cup heavy cream or Heavy Cream Substitute (page 212)

salt and pepper

1 tablespoon breadcrumbs or cracker crumbs (optional)

1. In a medium saucepan, combine the peas, butter, and cream or substitute. Season to taste with salt and pepper. Over medium heat, bring the mixture to an active simmer, stirring frequently.

2. Remove from the heat. If you wish, add 1 tablespoon breadcrumbs or cracker crumbs to thicken the sauce.

Potato Croquettes

Serves 4

1½ cups water

4 cups instant potato flakes

2 tablespoons milk

¼ cup dehydrated onions

1 teaspoon garlic powder

½ teaspoon salt

¼ teaspoon pepper

3 dashes of Tabasco sauce (optional)

1 egg

1½ cups dry breadcrumbs

vegetable oil for frying

1. In a saucepan over high heat, bring the water to a rapid boil. Stir in the instant mashed potatoes. Add the milk and dehydrated onions, garlic powder, salt, pepper, and Tabasco sauce, stirring well until combined.

2. Using an ice cream scoop, form balls of mashed potatoes.

3. Beat the egg in a small bowl. Place the dry breadcrumbs in another small bowl or rimmed pan. Dip the potato balls in egg and then dredge in breadcrumbs.

4. Pour oil to a depth of 2 inches in a deep skillet. Heat the oil in the skillet over medium-high heat. Fry the potato balls in the oil until the breadcrumbs become golden brown, flipping to brown completely, about 3 to 4 minutes.

Un-fried Refried Beans

Un-fried refried beans are great served with rice as a main dish or side dish for a Tex-Mex meal. They also make a delicious filling for tortillas, or use them as a dip. Spice things up with hot sauce as desired. *Serves 4*

2 tablespoons dried onion flakes

2 tablespoons dried garlic flakes

2 tablespoons dried chopped bell pepper

¼ cup boiling water

1 (15.4-ounce) can pinto beans, rinsed and drained, or 1 cup dried pinto beans, cooked

3 tablespoons tomato paste

1 tablespoon chili powder

1 tablespoon ground cumin

salt, to taste

1. In a small bowl, combine the onion, garlic, and pepper. Pour the boiling water over the mixture.

2. While the vegetables are rehydrating, combine the other ingredients in a small saucepan over low heat, stirring frequently.

3. Stir in the rehydrated vegetables and continue to heat until warmed through.

Corn Fritters

Serves 6

2 cups cornmeal

2 eggs, lightly beaten

¾ cup all-purpose flour, sifted

½ teaspoon salt

1 tablespoon sugar

¼ teaspoon white pepper

1 teaspoon baking powder

vegetable oil, for frying

1. Mix together the cornmeal and eggs. Stir in the flour, salt, sugar, pepper, and baking powder.

2. Heat oil in a skillet over medium-high heat. Drop tablespoons of batter into the hot oil. Cook the fritters 2 to 4 minutes, or until golden on both sides, turning once.

Jessica's Sweet Kale Salad

Serves 4 to 6

1 bunch kale, chopped

½ cup raisins or dried cranberries

½ cup raw, unsalted shelled pumpkin seeds

1 unpeeled green apple, cored and diced

1 avocado, chopped

olive oil

Celtic sea salt, pepper, ground coriander, and ground cumin, to taste

Mix together the kale, raisins or cranberries, pumpkin seeds, apple, and avocado. Drizzle with olive oil. Season as you like with salt and pepper, coriander, and cumin. Toss gently to combine.

Baked Kale Chips

You can make a dehydrated version of kale chips the same way as this recipe—just dehydrate the kale until crispy rather than baking it. Store in a zip-top bag. *Makes 2 servings*

1 bunch kale

1 tablespoon olive oil

1 teaspoon seasoning salt

1 teaspoon red wine vinegar (optional)

1. Preheat the oven to 350°F. Line a baking sheet with parchment paper.

2. Using a knife or kitchen shears, cut the kale leaves from the thick stems. Tear into bite-size pieces. Wash and thoroughly dry the leaves, using a salad spinner.

2. Spread the kale on the prepared baking sheet and drizzle with the olive oil. Sprinkle with seasoning salt, and use a spray bottle to spritz the kale with the red wine vinegar, if using.

3. Bake until the edges of the kale have browned but aren't burnt, 10 to 15 minutes. Store the baked chips in an airtight container.

Baked Potato Chips

Serves 4 to 6

5 to 6 unpeeled russet potatoes, very thinly sliced (about 4 pounds)

¼ cup olive oil

1 tablespoon chili powder or other seasoning (such as ranch dressing mix or Italian seasoning)

salt and pepper

1. Preheat the oven to 400°F. Spray two rimmed baking sheets with cooking spray.

2. Boil the potato slices in water, uncovered, for 8 minutes; drain.

3. In a large bowl, combine the olive oil and chili powder or other seasoning, and mix until incorporated. Add the potatoes to the bowl and gently toss to coat.

4. Spread the potato slices in a single layer on each prepared baking sheet. Cook for 10 to 15

minutes and then flip the slices over. Bake for an additional 10 to 15 minutes.

5. Let the potato chips cool for 10 minutes before serving.

Hominy Casserole

Serves 4

3 tablespoons unsalted butter

1 cup chopped onion

2 (15-ounce) cans hominy, undrained

1 (4-ounce) can chopped green chiles, rinsed and drained

½ pound Velveeta, cubed or ¾ cup dehydrated sharp Cheddar cheese

1 cup sour cream

½ teaspoon ground cumin

2 garlic cloves, minced

½ cup rehydrated meat crumbles, such as ham or ground beef (optional)

salt and pepper

1. Preheat the oven to 350°F.

2. In a large skillet over medium heat, melt the butter and sauté the onions until soft. Add hominy in a saucepan over medium heat until the liquid from the can has evaporated. Add salt and pepper.

3. Mix in the chiles, cheese, sour cream, seasonings and meat crumbles (if using). Pour into an ungreased 1.8-liter casserole dish and bake for 30 minutes.

Mashed Potatoes

Serves 4 to 5

3 to 5 red or russet potatoes (about 6 pounds), peeled

1 to 2 tablespoons butter

½ cup milk

½ teaspoon salt

1. Cook the potatoes in a large pot of boiling water over medium-high heat, ensuring that all the potatoes are covered. Cook the

potatoes until soft, and drain in a colander.

2. Add the butter to the potatoes and mash with a potato masher.

3. Pour milk into potatoes and add the salt, continuing to mash potatoes.

4. Mash until potatoes are smooth. Serve warm.

Green Bean Salad

Serves 4

¼ cup olive oil

3 tablespoons red wine vinegar

1½ teaspoons Dijon mustard

1 teaspoon salt

¼ teaspoon pepper

3 cups cooked green beans

½ cup chopped fresh basil leaves

1 tablespoon Italian seasoning

4 ounces feta cheese, crumbled

In a small bowl, whisk together the olive oil, vinegar, mustard, salt, and pepper. Place the green beans and remaining ingredients in a medium bowl and pour the dressing over them; toss well.

Poppaw's Turnip Greens

Serves 6

1 pound turnip greens

5 or 6 turnip roots, peeled and quartered (about 3 pounds)

juice of 1 lemon

1 onion, chopped

4 bacon slices, cooked and chopped, drippings reserved

salt and pepper

1. Rinse the turnip greens several times to remove any grit and tear the leaves into bite-size pieces.

2. Place the turnip roots and greens in a large pot and fill halfway with water. (The greens will greatly reduce in volume while cooking, so don't use too much water.) Add the lemon juice.

3. Place the chopped onion, chopped bacon, and bacon drippings in the pot with the turnips and greens.

4. Cook over medium heat, covered, until the turnips are tender, about 30 minutes. Season with salt and pepper to taste.

Personal Eggplant Marinara

Serves 4 to 6

2 or 3 small eggplants (2 to 3 pounds)

olive oil, as needed

1 (24-ounce) jar marinara sauce or 5 cups homemade Spaghetti Meat Sauce (page 70)

1 cup grated Parmesan cheese

1 to 2 tablespoons Italian seasoning

1. Preheat the oven to 375°F.

2. Cut the eggplants into ½-inch-thick slices. Brush the eggplant

with olive oil and sprinkle with Italian seasoning.

3. Spoon marinara sauce into the bottom of a large baking dish, and arrange the eggplant slices in the dish. Top each slice with 1 or 2 spoonfuls of marinara sauce and sprinkle on the cheese.

4. Bake for 20 minutes, covered, or until the cheese is golden brown and the eggplant is soft.

Mixed Vegetables with Dijon Mustard Sauce

Serves 4 to 5

4 cups mixed fresh vegetables (such as broccoli, cauliflower, carrots, and asparagus)

salt and pepper

1 cup sour cream

2 tablespoons red wine vinegar

¼ cup Dijon mustard

2 teaspoons sugar

⅛ teaspoon cayenne pepper

1. Steam the vegetables for 4 to 5 minutes, to the desired degree of doneness.

2. Meanwhile, whisk together the remaining ingredients in a small saucepan. Warm the sauce over low heat until it just begins to simmer.

3. Serve the sauce with the cooked vegetables.

Broccoli-Cauliflower Medley with Cheese Sauce

Makes 4 servings

1 tablespoon butter

1 tablespoon all-purpose flour

1 cup half and half or Heavy Cream Substitute (page 212)

1½ cup cubed Velveeta cheese or ½ cup dehydrated shredded sharp Cheddar cheese (1-inch cubes)

salt and pepper

½ teaspoon garlic powder

⅛ teaspoon paprika

4 cups cooked broccoli and cauliflower florets

1. In a skillet over medium heat, melt the butter and whisk in the flour.

2. Gradually whisk in the half and half or cream substitute and bring to an active simmer. Whisk until smooth.

3. Add the Velveeta and seasonings and continue to stir until the cheese is melted and completely incorporated.

4. Pour the sauce over the vegetables just before serving.

Sweet Potato Bake

Serves 4 to 6

3 sweet potatoes, mashed

¼ cup milk

2 teaspoons vanilla extract

½ cup packed brown sugar

¼ teaspoon salt

PECAN CRUMBLE TOPPING

½ cup finely chopped pecans

½ cup packed brown sugar

3 tablespoons all-purpose flour

¼ cup (½ stick) butter, softened

1. Preheat the oven to 375°F.

2. Combine the sweet potatoes, milk, vanilla, brown sugar, and salt; mix well. Transfer to a lightly greased baking dish.

3. Work the topping ingredients together to form a crumbly mixture. Sprinkle over the sweet potato mixture.

4. Bake, uncovered, for 25 minutes..

Stuffed Spaghetti Squash

Serves 3 to 4

1 spaghetti squash, halved and seeded (about 2 pounds)

1 (15.5-ounce) can white beans, drained and rinsed

1 (15.5-ounce) can black-eyed peas, drained and rinsed

1 garlic clove, minced

¾ teaspoon salt

3 tablespoons balsamic vinegar

1 tablespoon Dijon mustard

1 teaspoon honey

3 tablespoons olive oil

1½ tablespoons Italian seasoning

1. Preheat the oven to 375°F. In a large baking dish, arrange the squash halves and pour in 1-inch of water. Bake for 45 minutes, or until tender.

2. In a 4-quart saucepan over medium-high heat, combine the beans, garlic, and black-eyed peas and heat through.

3. In a small bowl, whisk together the vinegar, mustard, honey, olive oil, and Italian seasoning.

4. Using a fork, loosen the squash pulp from the shell. Top with the bean mixture and drizzle the balsamic vinaigrette over the top.

Creamed Corn and Carrots

Makes 5 servings

1 tablespoon olive oil

2 medium red potatoes, diced

1 carrot, peeled and chopped

½ medium onion, diced

2 cups water

2 (8.5-ounce) cans cream-style corn, undrained

1½ teaspoons salt

pepper

½ cup milk

½ cup cooked diced bacon or bacon bits

1. In a large sauté pan over medium heat, add the olive oil and sauté the potatoes, carrot, and onion until the onion pieces are soft.

2. Add the water, corn, salt, and pepper and simmer for 20 minutes.

3. Stir in the milk and bacon pieces and bring to an active simmer.

Zucchini Boats

Serves 6

3 zucchini squash halved lengthwise

3 tablespoons olive oil

½ cup shredded mozzarella cheese

¾ teaspoon dried basil

½ teaspoon Italian seasoning

2 garlic cloves, minced

2 tablespoons dried onion flakes

2 or 3 small tomatoes, thinly sliced

¼ cup dry breadcrumbs

¼ cup grated Parmesan cheese

salt and pepper

1. Preheat the oven to 350°F.

2. With a spoon, scrape out the seeds from the zucchini halves.

3. Place the zucchini halves on a baking sheet and coat with olive oil. Sprinkle on the mozzarella cheese, basil, Italian seasoning, garlic, onion flakes, salt, and pepper.

4. Arrange tomato slices on the zucchini. Top with the breadcrumbs and Parmesan cheese.

5. Bake for 25 minutes, or until the tops are golden.

Onion Gratin

Makes 4 servings

2 large yellow onions, cut into
¼-inch slices

1 tablespoon olive oil

1 cup dry breadcrumbs

salt and pepper

3 tablespoons dried thyme

1 tablespoon butter

1 tablespoon all-purpose flour

1 cup Heavy Cream Substitute (page 212)

¼ teaspoon garlic powder

¼ cup white wine

½ cup grated Parmesan cheese

1. Preheat the oven to 375°F.

2. Spread the onions on a rimmed baking sheet and drizzle with the olive oil. Coat with the breadcrumbs, season with salt and pepper to taste, and sprinkle with thyme. Bake for 15 minutes.

3. Meanwhile, make a roux by melting the butter in a medium sauté pan over medium heat and whisking in the flour. Add the heavy cream substitute and garlic powder and whisk until the mixture thickens. Add the wine and stir until the mixture bubbles.

4. Transfer the onions to a 4-quart baking dish and spoon the cream sauce onto them. Top with the Parmesan cheese. Cover with foil and bake for 35 minutes, or until the top is golden brown.

5. When ready to serve, drizzle the sauce in the dish over the onions.

Tomatoes Balsamico

This side dish is great cooked or uncooked! To make it more filling, spread a few spoonfuls of fresh ricotta or farmer's cheese over the tomatoes before topping them with the other ingredients. Add a spoonful of marinara sauce to each serving. *Makes 6 (2-slice) servings*

3 or 4 medium to large tomatoes, thickly sliced

3 tablespoons balsamic vinaigrette dressing (recipe follows)

1 garlic clove, minced

¼ cup grated Parmesan cheese

1 tablespoon dried or 2 tablespoons fresh basil

salt and pepper

1. Preheat the oven to 400°F.

2. Spread the tomatoes on a baking sheet lined with foil. Brush with the vinaigrette, and sprinkle on the garlic and Parmesan cheese. Add the salt and pepper to taste.

3. Top with basil and roast for 20 minutes.

Balsamic Vinaigrette Dressing

Makes 6 servings

¼ cup extra virgin olive oil

¼ cup red balsamic vinegar

1 clove garlic, minced

1 teaspoon prepared mustard

1 teaspoon Italian seasoning

salt and pepper

In a medium bowl, add oil and vinegar and aggressively stir until combined. Add remaining ingredients and stir until mixed.

10 GRAINS

A savory side dish of grains can really help fill out a meal, elevating the simplest main dish meat to the status of "dinner" and adding an energizing serving of inexpensive carbohydrates. This is a great way to extend your food supply!

Creamy Risotto-Style Rice

For a complete meal, add dehydrated meat strips and vegetables while rice is steaming. *Serves 5 to 6*

1 tablespoon olive oil

1 cup minced onion

2 garlic cloves, minced

1¼ cups uncooked white rice

3 tablespoons white wine

2½ cups water

2 cups milk

1 medium tomato, peeled, seeded, and chopped

1⅓ cups fresh or dehydrated corn kernels

1 teaspoon Italian seasoning

½ teaspoon salt

freshly ground pepper, to taste

½ cup grated Parmesan cheese

1. Heat the oil in a large sauté pan, over medium heat. Sauté the onion and garlic in the oil until soft.

2. Add the rice and toast over medium heat for 2 minutes. Stir to prevent from burning.

3. Stir in the white wine.

4. Add the water, milk, tomato, corn, Italian seasoning, salt, and

pepper. Heat until the mixture comes to an active simmer.

5. Cover, reduce the heat to low, and cook for 15 minutes. Then turn off the heat but leave the rice on the burner, covered, for 10 more minutes.

6. Stir in the Parmesan cheese and serve warm.

Rice and Broccoli Casserole

To turn this comforting casserole into a complete meal, simply add a 12.5-ounce can of chuck chicken. *Serves 4 to 6*

2 cups fresh or frozen broccoli florets, thawed

1 cup shredded sharp Cheddar cheese or Cheez Whiz, or 1 (10.75-ounce) can condensed Cheddar cheese soup, plus more (optional) for sprinkling

1 cup condensed cream of mushroom soup

¾ cup milk

1 cup uncooked instant rice or 2 cups cooked rice

salt and pepper

1. Preheat the oven to 350°F.

2. Mix all the ingredients together in a large bowl. Pour the mixture into a greased casserole dish. If you have it, sprinkle additional cheese on top.

3. Cover with a casserole lid or foil. Bake for 45 minutes if you are using uncooked instant rice. If you're using cooked rice, bake until the dish is hot all the way through and the cheese is bubbly, about 30 minutes.

Easy Cheesy Rice

You can use more cheese or a different type of cheese—adapt this to whatever you have on hand. *Serves 5*

4 cups water

2 teaspoons chicken bouillon granules

2 tablespoons butter or margarine

1½ cups uncooked medium-grain rice

3 slices American cheese

1. In a 4-quart saucepan over medium-high heat, bring the water, boullion granules, and butter to a boil.

2. Stir in the rice, cover, and reduce the heat to low. Cook for 15 to 20 minutes or until the rice is tender, adding more water if needed.

3. Remove from the heat, tear the cheese into small pieces, and stir it into the rice until completely melted.

Baked Brown Rice

Brown rice can be time-consuming to prepare. Spare your fuel and use this recipe when you have something else to go into the oven at a similar heat. *Serves 5*

2½ cups broth, or 2½ cups water with 1 chicken or beef bouillon cube

1½ cups brown rice and wild rice mixture

2 garlic cloves, finely minced

salt and pepper

1. Preheat the oven to 375°F.

2. In a 3-quart oven-safe saucepan, bring the broth (or water and bouillon cube) to a boil over medium heat.

3. Add the rice, garlic, and salt and pepper to taste; immediately put the lid on to seal the pot tightly.

4. Place in the oven and bake for exactly 1 hour and you'll have a pot of perfect fluffy rice.

Quick Rice Pilaf

Serves 4

1 cup water

1 tablespoon chicken or beef bouillon granules

1 (15-ounce) can peas and carrots or mixed vegetables

1 cup uncooked instant rice

1. In a 4-quart saucepan over medium-high heat, bring the water, bouillon, and veggies to a boil.

2. Stir in the rice.

3. Cover, remove from the heat, and let sit for 5 minutes. Fluff with a fork and serve.

Pepper-Oat Pilaf

Serves 4

1 to 2 tablespoons vegetable oil

½ cup chopped roasted red peppers (canned or fresh)

1 (4.5-ounce) can sliced mushrooms, drained or ½ cup sliced fresh mushrooms

1¾ cups rolled oats

1 egg, beaten well

1 tablespoon dried minced onion

1 tablespoon dried minced garlic

¾ cup broth

2 tablespoons dried thyme

salt and pepper

grated Parmesan cheese, for serving (optional)

1. Heat the oil in a large saucepan over medium heat. Sauté the peppers and mushrooms in the oil until they are starting to brown slightly.

2. In a medium bowl, stir together the oats, egg, onion, and garlic until the oats are coated.

3. Stir the oats into the mixture in the saucepan and cook, stirring frequently, until the oats are dry and separated, 5 to 10 minutes.

4. Stir in the broth, thyme, and salt and pepper to taste; cook for a few more minutes, stirring until the liquid has been absorbed.

5. Sprinkle with Parmesan cheese, if you wish, and serve hot.

Basic Wheat Berries

Serves 4

1 cup dry wheat berries

1 teaspoon salt

3½ cups water

1. Sort through the wheat berries, discarding any stones. Rinse well.

2. In a large saucepan over medium heat, bring the wheat berries, water, and salt to a boil.

3. Reduce the heat to low, cover, and simmer for 1 hour, or until the wheat berries are tender. (Undercooked wheat berries have an unpleasant texture—make sure you've cooked them thoroughly!)

As mentioned in "Making Meals Stretch" (page 28), wheat berries are one of those healthy, multipurpose preps that can help sustain us during long-term emergencies. They can be eaten as a breakfast cereal, ground into wheat flour, used to make bread, added to soups, cooked, added to salads, sprouted for a healthy snack, and even sweetened for desserts. They are also a true whole grain. One cup of cooked wheat berries has about 300 calories and is packed with fiber, protein, and iron. Tasty sprouts are loaded with vitamin E, a cell-protecting antioxidant, and magnesium, which is good for healthy bones and muscles. In an extended emergency, having a diet that is calorie and vitamin rich will help you withstand the increased physical demands of surviving a long-term disaster, as well as keep you healthy.

Wheat berries can be purchased at your local natural food store, in the organic section of your grocery store, through the Latter Day Saints distribution warehouse in your area, on emergency preparedness websites, or through bulk food websites.

Wheat Berry Rice Pilaf

Serves 6

2 teaspoons olive oil

1 (4-ounce) can sliced mushrooms, drained or ½ cup sliced fresh mushrooms

1 tablespoon soy sauce

1 tablespoon dried minced onion

1 tablespoon dried minced garlic

1½ cups cooked Basic Wheat Berries (page 170)

1½ cups cooked brown or white rice

½ cup beef or chicken broth

1 tablespoon dried thyme

salt and pepper

1. Heat the oil in a large saucepan over medium heat. Sauté the mushrooms in the oil until soft, about 3 minutes.

2. Sprinkle the mushrooms with the soy sauce, then stir in the onion and garlic. Cook for 2 more minutes, stirring constantly.

3. Stir in the rest of the ingredients and cook for 5 to 10 minutes, stirring, until the broth has been absorbed and the pilaf is heated through.

Wheat Berry Cranberry Salad

Prepare this recipe a day ahead for the best flavor. *Serves 8*

2 cups cooked Basic Wheat Berries (page 170)

½ cup walnuts, chopped

½ cup fresh parsley, coarsely chopped

½ cup dried cranberries

4 tablespoons dehydrated green onions or ¼ cup sliced fresh green onions, sliced (optional)

dash of salt

DRESSING

3 tablespoons olive oil

2 tablespoons lemon juice

1 teaspoon honey

salt and pepper

1. In a large bowl, mix together all the salad ingredients.

2. In a small bowl, whisk together the dressing ingredients. Pour the dressing over the salad and gently toss. Refrigerate the dressed salad to allow the flavors to meld before serving.

Santa Fe Rice Salad

Serves 3 to 4

- 1½ cups cooked white rice
- 1 cup canned black beans, drained
- ½ cup canned whole kernel corn, drained
- 1 cup diced tomatoes
- ½ cup shredded Cheddar cheese (optional)

DRESSING

- ¼ cup distilled white vinegar
- ¼ cup vegetable oil
- 1 tablespoon lemon juice
- 1 teaspoon chili powder
- 1 teaspoon granulated sugar
- 1 tablespoon diced jalapeño chiles (optional)

1. In a large bowl, stir together the rice, beans, corn, and tomatoes. Chill in the refrigerator for 20 minutes.

2. In a small bowl, whisk together the dressing ingredients. Pour the dressing over the chilled salad and stir gently to combine.

3. Sprinkle with shredded Cheddar cheese, if using.

Basic Quinoa

The trick to delicious, lightly sweet quinoa is washing it well to remove its bitter coating. Rinse the quinoa in a mesh strainer under running water until the water is clear, not frothy. If running water isn't available, "swish" the quinoa in a large bowl of water and drain well. Use fresh water for cooking it. Quinoa can be used wherever you'd normally use rice or pasta—under sauces or stir-fries, as a side dish, even as a hot breakfast cereal. It's all a matter of how you season it. *Serves 4*

- 2 cups water
- 1 cup quinoa

1. Rinse the quinoa and drain well.

2. In a medium saucepan over medium-high heat, bring the water to a boil. Add the quinoa, reduce the heat to low, cover, and simmer for 15 minutes.

3. Remove from the heat, place the lid on the pan, and let sit for 5 minutes. Fluff with a fork before serving.

Quinoa Pilaf

Serves 4

1 cup quinoa

2 cups water

2 cubes chicken or vegetable bouillon

¼ cup dehydrated carrots

¼ cup dehydrated green or red bell peppers

2 tablespoons dried minced onion

½ teaspoon dried oregano

salt and pepper

¼ cup dried cranberries

1. Rinse the quinoa and drain well.

2. In a medium saucepan over medium heat, combine the quinoa, water, and all remaining ingredients except for the cranberries. Bring to a boil, then reduce the heat to low, and simmer for 15 minutes, uncovered.

3. Remove from the heat and stir in the cranberries. Place the lid on the pan and let sit for 5 minutes. Fluff with a fork before serving.

Quinoa Tabouli

This Middle Eastern salad is easily made from pantry ingredients.

Serves 5 to 6

2 cups cooked Basic Quinoa (page 172)

½ cup dried parsley

½ cup sliced green onions or 1 teaspoon onion powder

1 teaspoon garlic powder

1 tablespoon dried mint

½ teaspoon basil

½ cup lemon juice

¼ cup olive oil

salt and pepper

Greek seasoning

1. Place the quinoa in a large bowl. Lightly stir in the remaining ingredients until mixed.

2. Cover and refrigerate for at least 12 hours to allow the flavors to meld. Serve chilled.

Uncle Terry's Cheese Grits

Serves 4 to 5

1 cup uncooked plain grits

8 ounces Cheez Whiz or Velveeta, diced

¼ cup (½ stick) unsalted butter

¾ teaspoon salt

¼ teaspoon garlic salt

2 eggs, lightly beaten

1. Prepare the grits according to the package directions.

2. While the grits are cooking, preheat the oven to 350°F. Grease an 8 x 8-inch baking dish.

3. Stir the remaining ingredients into the hot grits until the cheese and butter are melted. Pour into the prepared dish and bake for 35 to 40 minutes.

Mexican Rice

Serves 5

½ cup uncooked white rice

1 small onion, chopped, or ⅓ cup dehydrated onion

1 garlic clove, minced

1 tablespoon butter or vegetable oil

1 cup beef broth, or 1 cup water and 1 beef bouillon cube

1 cup canned diced tomatoes

1 (4-ounce) can diced green chiles, chopped

2 teaspoons ground cumin

salt and pepper

1 teaspoon chili powder

1. In a large skillet over medium heat, sauté the rice, onion, and garlic in the butter or oil until golden brown.

2. Add the beef broth or water and bouillon. Stir in the tomatoes, chiles, cumin, salt, pepper, and chili powder.

3. Cover and cook over low heat for 25 to 30 minutes, or until the rice is tender.

Cornbread Salad

Serves 9

1 (9 x 13-inch) pan cooked cornbread, crumbled

1 cup chopped celery

½ cup chopped onion

3 hard-cooked eggs, chopped

1 green bell pepper, chopped

½ cup bacon bits or 4 cooked bacon slices, drained and crumbled

1 or 2 tomatoes, chopped

1½ cups mayonnaise

salt and pepper

1 (1-ounce) packet ranch dressing mix (optional)

Gently toss all the ingredients together in a large bowl. If using the ranch dressing mix, no additional salt and pepper is needed. Cover and refrigerate to serve chilled.

Bread and biscuits can go a long way toward making any simple fare more filling. And they have the added bonus of helping you get that last little bit of delicious soup or sauce at the bottom of your bowl!

Yeast Biscuits

Makes 8

- 2 tablespoons sugar
- 1 cup warm water (110°F)
- 1 packet (2¼ teaspoons) active dry yeast
- 2 cups all-purpose flour
- ½ cup nonfat dry milk
- ¼ teaspoon salt
- ½ cup vegetable shortening

1. In a small bowl, stir together the sugar, warm water, and yeast. Let stand for 10 to 15 minutes.

2. In a large bowl, mix together the flour, powdered milk, and salt. Cut in the shortening using a fork. Stir in the yeast mixture.

Cover bowl with a towel and allow it to rest for 1 hour. Dough should be very sticky.

3. After the dough has risen, scrape it out onto a well-floured surface and knead for 4 minutes then roll out and shape into 8 biscuits.

4. Place the biscuits on a greased baking sheet and cover with a clean dish cloth to allow to rise until nearly doubled in size, 30 to 45 minutes. Meanwhile, preheat the oven to 400°F.

5. Bake the biscuits for 10 to 12 minutes, until lightly browned.

Quick Buttermilk Biscuits

Makes 8

½ cup (1 stick) butter

2 cups self-rising flour

¾ cup buttermilk

2 tablespoons melted butter, for brushing

1. Preheat the oven to 425°F. Lightly grease a 9 x 9-inch baking pan.

2. In a medium bowl, work the butter into the flour until the mixture resembles coarse meal. Add the buttermilk, stirring just until the flour mixture is moistened.

3. Turn the dough out onto a lightly floured surface and knead 3 or 4 times. Roll to a ¾ inch thickness; cut with a 2-inch biscuit cutter. Place the biscuits on the prepared pan.

4. Bake for 13 to 15 minutes, until tops are golden. Brush the tops of the hot biscuits with melted butter and serve warm.

Pop's Beer Bread

Makes 1 loaf

3 cups self-rising flour

1 tablespoon granulated sugar

2 tablespoons honey

1 (12-ounce) bottle of beer

1. Set the oven to its lowest setting. Grease a 9 x 5-inch bread pan.

2. Place all the ingredients in a large bowl and mix together with a spoon. Pour into the prepared bread pan and place, uncovered, in the warm oven for 15 minutes.

3. Increase temperature to 375°F and bake for 40 minutes. Allow to cool for 15 minutes on a wire rack.

Cornbread

Serves 8

1 egg, beaten

2 tablespoons butter, melted

1 cup milk

¾ cup cornmeal

1 cup all-purpose flour

¼ cup granulated sugar

1 tablespoon baking powder

½ teaspoon salt

1. Preheat the oven to 425°F. Grease an 8 x 8-inch baking pan.

2. Mix the egg, butter, and milk in a small bowl. Set aside.

3. In a separate bowl, stir together the cornmeal, flour, sugar, baking powder, and salt. Beat in the milk mixture. Spread evenly in the prepared pan.

4. Bake for 20 minutes. Allow to cool for 10 minutes on a wire rack before serving.

Quick and Easy Corn Muffins

Makes 8 servings

⅓ cup baking mix (such as Bisquick)

1 cup yellow cornmeal

6 tablespoons granulated sugar

⅔ cup milk

2 eggs

1. Preheat the oven to 400°F. Grease an 9 x 13-inch pan or 8 cups of a standard muffin tin.

2. Whisk together the baking mix, cornmeal, and sugar in a bowl. Add the milk and eggs, stirring until the lumps are gone.

3. Pour the mixture into the prepared baking pan or fill the muffin cups half full. Bake 15 to 20 minutes, or until the muffin tops are slightly browned. If using a 9 x 13-inch pan to cook the cornbread, bake for 20 to 25 minutes or until a toothpick inserted into the cornbread comes out clean. Remove from the oven and let it cool slightly on a wire rack and serve warm.

Tip: For a sweet addition to your corn muffins, sauté ½ cup minced dried or fresh fruit (peaches, pineapple, mango, apples, or cranberries) in 3 tablespoons butter for 5 minutes to use as a tasty spread.

Butter Biscuits

To make garlic cheese biscuits, add ½ teaspoon garlic powder and 1¼ cups grated Cheddar cheese to the batter. *Makes 8*

2½ cups Bisquick baking mix

dash of salt

¼ cup (½ stick) cold unsalted butter, cubed

¾ cup cold milk

1. Preheat the oven to 400°F.

2. Using a large fork, combine the Bisquick and salt with the cold butter in a medium bowl. Small chunks of butter should remain, about the size of peas. Stir in the milk until combined, but don't overmix.

3. Drop ¼-cup portions of dough onto an ungreased baking sheet, using an ice cream scoop.

4. Bake for 15 to 17 minutes, or until the tops of the biscuits begin to turn light brown.

No-Knead Bread

Makes 1 loaf

3 cups all-purpose flour

¼ teaspoon active dry yeast

½ teaspoon salt

1 tablespoon sugar

1½ cups warm water (110°F)

1. In a large bowl, mix all the ingredients together until well incorporated (the dough will be very soft and sticky). Cover with plastic wrap or put in an airtight container and let sit for 18 hours. (My microwave serves as the resting spot for this step.)

2. After the 18 hours, place the dough on a floured surface. Dampen your hands with a little water (this keeps the dough from sticking to you) and knead for 4 minutes. Shape the dough into a ball.

3. Transfer the dough to a lightly greased 9-inch baking dish or Dutch oven with a lid. Allow the dough to rest for another 1½ to 2 hours or until it begins to rise again.

4. Preheat the oven to 500°F. Bake, covered, for 30 minutes. Remove the lid and reduce the oven temperature to 450°F. Bake an additional 15 minutes, until golden brown and the center is hollow when tapped.

5. Allow to cool completely on a wire rack.

Simple Wheat Bread

Makes 2 loaves

4 teaspoons active dry yeast

2 cups warm water (110°F)

⅓ cup granulated sugar

⅓ cup honey

3 tablespoons olive oil

5 cups whole wheat flour (or 3 cups whole wheat flour and 2 cups all-purpose flour)

1. Stir the yeast into the warm water in a small bowl. Set aside to let the yeast activate, about 10 minutes.

2. In a large bowl, stir together the sugar, honey, and olive oil. Add the flour and yeast mixture and mix thoroughly.

3. Transfer the dough to a lightly greased bowl, cover with a dishtowel, and allow the dough to rest and rise in a warm place until doubled in size, about 2 hours (I set mine inside my microwave). After the dough has risen, punch it down and then knead it for about 2 minutes. Shape it into 2 loaves. Place in lightly greased 9 x 5-inch loaf pans.

4. Allow the loaves to rest in the unheated oven for another hour.

Place a bowl of hot water in the oven to help the dough rise faster.

5. Remove the bread and bowl of hot water, and preheat the oven to 400°F. Bake the loaves for 30 minutes.

White Bread

Makes 1 loaf

2 packets (4½ teaspoons) active dry yeast

2 tablespoons granulated sugar

1 cup warm water (110°F)

2 teaspoons salt

5 cups all-purpose flour, divided

1½ cups warm milk (110°F),

½ teaspoon baking soda dissolved in 1 tablespoon water

cornmeal, for bread pan

1. In a large bowl, dissolve the yeast and sugar in the water. Set aside for 15 minutes to let the yeast activate.

2. After 15 minutes, beat in the salt, 3 cups of the flour, and 1 cup of the milk. Stir in the dissolved baking soda until well blended.

3. Beat in the remaining ½ cup milk and 1½ to 2 cups more flour, to make a stiff dough. Mix until the dough becomes too sticky to mix with a spoon (about 3 minutes).

4. Allow bread to rise covered in a warm place for 2 hours or until it has doubled in size. On a lightly floured surface, knead the dough for 5 minutes.

5. Grease a 9 x 5-inch loaf pan and coat with cornmeal. Shape the dough into a loaf and place in the pan. Cover and let rise in a warm place for 45 to 60 minutes, until doubled in size.

6. Preheat the oven to 375°F. Once the bread has risen, bake for 25 to 30 minutes, or until the top of the loaf is golden brown.

Poor Man's Village Bread

This is extremely adaptable bread that can be baked, pan-fried, or grilled. Additional ingredients can also be added according to your taste. This specialty bread can be served with soup, as an addition to any meal, or on its own for a snack. *Serves 8 to 10*

2 cups sauerkraut, drained

1 cup all-purpose flour

¾ teaspoon salt

optional additions: sprouts, diced peppers, finely chopped herbs, caraway seeds, chopped garlic, julienned spinach

olive oil, for greasing pan

1. Preheat the oven to 350°F. Grease a baking sheet with olive oil.

2. Mix the sauerkraut and flour together to make a sticky dough. If the dough seems too dry, add 1 to 2 tablespoons water or sauerkraut liquid until you have the desired consistency.

3. Add the salt and any optional additions and mix until dough stays at a sticky consistency.

4. Flour your hands and shape the dough into small flattened balls about the size of the palms of your hands. Repeat until all dough has been used.

5. Place the flattened dough balls on the prepared baking sheet and use a fork to poke holes in the tops so steam can escape.

6. Bake for 6 to 8 minutes and then turn to cook on the second side. If you wish, when you flip the bread over you can sprinkle on a desired amount of flavorings or spices such as garlic, spinach, or herbs, or drizzle on olive oil.

7. Bake for an additional 6 to 8 minutes. Serve warm.

Oat Rolls

These delicious rolls can be served with whipped honey butter.

Makes 18

2½ cups water, divided

1 cup rolled oats

⅔ cup packed dark brown sugar

3 tablespoons butter

1¾ teaspoons salt

2 tablespoons active dry yeast

5 to 6 cups all-purpose flour

1. In a 4-quart saucepan over medium heat, bring 2 of the cups of the water to a boil. Stir in the oats and reduce the heat to a simmer until oats are soft. Remove from the heat and allow to cool until it reaches 110°F.

2. Stir in the remaining ½ cup water and the brown sugar, butter, and salt. Stir in the yeast. Let rest for 15 minutes and then stir in the flour, 1 cup at a time. Mix until all the flour has been absorbed and the dough is smooth and elastic.

3. Place the dough in a greased bowl and cover with a towel. Let the dough rise in a warm place until doubled, about 1 hour, then punch it down.

4. Shape the dough into rolls on a greased baking sheet and cover; allowing to rise for another 30 minutes in a warm place until it begins to rise again.

5. Preheat the oven to 350°F. When the rolls have risen, bake them for 15 to 20 minutes.

Ezekiel Bread

Makes 2 loaves

4 cups warm water (110°F)

1 cup honey

½ cup olive oil

2 (2¼-teaspoon) packets active dry yeast

2½ cups wheat berries

1½ cups spelt flour

½ cup barley

½ cup millet

¼ cup dry green lentils

2 tablespoons dried Great Northern beans

2 tablespoons dried kidney beans

2 tablespoons dried pinto beans

2 tablespoons salt

1. Grease two 9 x 5-inch loaf pans. Set aside.

2. In a large bowl, stir together the water, honey, olive oil, and yeast. Let sit for 10 minutes.

3. In a second large bowl, stir all of the grains and beans together until well mixed. Grind them in a hand-crank or electric flour mill. Add the fresh-milled flour and the salt to the yeast mixture; stir until well mixed, about 10 minutes. The dough will be like batter bread dough.

4. Pour the dough into the prepared pans. Cover and let rise in a warm place for about 1 hour, or until the loaves have risen to the tops of the pans.

5. Preheat the oven to 350°F. When the dough has finished rising, bake the loaves for 45 to 50 minutes, or until they are golden brown.

Corn Tortillas

Makes about 15

2 cups masa harina

½ teaspoon kosher salt

1½ cups hot water (110°F)

vegetable oil, for the griddle

1. In a medium bowl, mix together the masa harina, salt, and hot water until thoroughly combined. Turn the dough onto a lightly floured surface and knead until it is pliable and smooth.

Tip: If the dough is too sticky, add more masa harina; if it begins to dry out, sprinkle with water.

2 Cover the dough tightly with plastic wrap and let stand for 30 minutes at room temperature.

3. Coat a griddle or skillet with oil and heat over medium-high heat.

4. Measure out heaping table spoons of dough and roll them into balls. Cover with a plastic

bag or plastic wrap and roll them as flat as possible. The size can vary according to what you are using them for (tacos, burritos, etc.).

5. Working in batches, place the flattened tortillas on the hot, oiled griddle (or in the skillet) and cook for 2 to 3 minutes, until dark spots appear and the edges begin to curl upward. Then turn over and cook for another 20 seconds.

6. Transfer the cooked tortillas to a plate and cover with a towel to keep them warm while you finish cooking the remaining tortillas. You can place a paper towel or napkin in between tortillas to remove excess oil. Serve warm.

7. To store tortillas, wrap them in foil and place them in an airtight container. To reheat, place foil-wrapped tortillas into a 350°F oven for 10 minutes.

Jessica's Emergency Bread

Makes 1 loaf

2 cups self-rising flour

1 teaspoon nonfat dry milk

water, as needed

toppings of choice (see instructions)

1. Combine the flour and milk powder in a bowl. Mix in water until you have a smooth, elastic dough. Form into a ball.

2. Heat a lightly greased cast-iron skillet over medium heat.

3. Flatten the dough ball to about ½ inch thick and place in the hot skillet. Cook for 5 to 10 minutes, flipping it over several times.

4. Serve warm topped with butter, herbs, and garlic for a savory flavor, or with butter and reconstituted dried fruit for a sweet flavor.

Breadsticks

Makes 16

1½ cups warm water (110°F)

1 tablespoon active dry yeast

2 tablespoons granulated sugar

1 teaspoon salt

4 cups all-purpose flour

melted butter, for baking sheet and breadsticks

garlic powder, to taste

½ cup shredded Cheddar or mozzarella cheese and/or ¼ cup grated Parmesan cheese, or cinnamon and sugar

1. In a large bowl, mix together the warm water, yeast, and sugar. Let sit for 5 minutes.

2. Stir in the salt. Stir in the flour, 1 cup at a time, mixing well with your hands until the dough pulls away from the side of the bowl.

3. Grease the inside of a large bowl or spray with cooking spray. Place the dough in the bowl, turning it to grease all sides, and cover with a damp towel.

4. Allow the dough to rise in a warm place for 20 minutes or until doubled in size. Butter a baking sheet.

5. Place the dough on a floured work surface and knead it for 2 to 5 minutes. Roll the dough to ¼ inch thickness.

6. Cut the dough into 1 to 2-inch-wide slices and transfer them to the prepared baking sheet. Brush with melted butter and dust with garlic powder. If you wish, sprinkle Cheddar, mozzarella, Parmesan cheese, or cinnamon and sugar on top of the breadsticks.

7. Allow the breadsticks to rise, covered, for another 20 minutes in a warm place. Meanwhile, preheat the oven to 375°F.

8. Bake for 15 minutes. Transfer the breadsticks to a wire rack to cool.

Potato Bread

Makes 1 loaf

1 cup unseasoned mashed potatoes (you can make them with instant flakes)

2 teaspoons active dry yeast

2½ tablespoons sugar

1 cup warm water

3 cups all-purpose flour

1 teaspoon salt

1. Preheat the oven to 375°F. Grease a bread pan or baking sheet, depending on whether you are making a single loaf or buns.

2. In a large bowl, beat together the mashed potatoes, yeast, sugar, and water until no lumps remain.

3. Sift together the flour and salt. Mix into the potato mixture.

4. On a floured surface, knead the dough until it is smooth. Form into a loaf or individual buns and transfer to the prepared pan or baking sheet.

5. Bake until the bread starts to brown, about 35 minutes for a loaf or 25 minutes for buns. Let cool on a wire rack.

Homemade Flour Tortillas

Because of the shortening in the dough, it's usually not necessary to use oil for "frying" these tortillas. If you notice any sticking, use a small amount of cooking spray or oil. *Makes 12 tortillas*

3 cups all-purpose flour, plus more for rolling

2 teaspoons baking powder

1 teaspoon salt

4 to 6 tablespoons vegetable shortening

1¼ cups warm water (110°F)

1. Mix the dry ingredients in a large bowl. Cut in the shortening, using a fork or pastry blender (or your clean hands).

2. Add warm water, a little at a time, until your dough is soft but not sticky.

3. Working on a floured surface, knead the dough for a couple of minutes. Divide into 12 balls and cover, allowing dough to rest for 10 to 15 minutes.

4. Heat a skillet over medium-high heat.

5. Dust each ball of dough with a little flour, then roll it into a fairly thin (about ⅛ inch thick), 3 to 4-inch round tortilla. If you don't have a rolling pin, you can use a glass or even your hands to shape the dough.

6. Lay the tortilla in the hot skillet. Watch carefully—it only takes a few seconds to cook. Flip the tortilla to the other side. You know it's done when you see many brown spots. Place the cooked tortillas on top of one another on a plate and cover with a clean dishtowel until ready to serve.

Homemade Baked Tortilla Chips

Makes 16 chips

4 flour tortillas corn tortillas or wheat tortillas, quartered

2 tablespoons vegetable oil, or cooking spray

salt, to taste

1. Preheat the oven to 350°F. Lightly brush oil onto a baking sheet.

2. Brush a light coating of oil on one side of each tortilla. Sprinkle with salt.

3. Stack the tortillas, greased side up, in an even pile. Cut in half, then in quarters, then in eighths. Separate and arrange the pieces, greased side up, on the prepared baking sheet.

4. Toast the chips in the oven for about 10 minutes, or until they are crisp and just beginning to brown lightly. Serve immediately or store in an airtight container.

Pizza Dough

Makes 1 pie or 8 servings

3 cups all-purpose flour

1 (2¼-tablespoons) packet active
   dry yeast

1 teaspoon salt

1 tablespoon sugar

2 tablespoons vegetable oil

1 cup warm water (110°F)

pizza toppings of choice

1. In a large bowl, combine the flour, yeast, salt, sugar, and warm water.

2. Add the oil to the bowl. Stir until the dough is well mixed. Transfer to a lightly oiled large bowl; cover and allow to rest in a warm place until doubled, about 90 minutes.

3. Preheat the oven to 375°F. Grease a large pizza pan.

4. Working on a floured surface, knead the dough and shape it. Roll the dough into a ball and allow to rest, covered, for 30 additional minutes. Transfer the dough to your work surface, lightly sprinkled with cornmeal. Shape the dough with lightly floured hands into a 9-inch disk, about ¼ inch thick. Brush the outer edge lightly with olive oil. Top as desired. Bake until the crust is golden brown, and the cheese is bubbling, 8 to 12 minutes.

Pita Bread

For pita chips, brush the cooked pita bread with oil, cut into quarters and bake at 375°F until crispy. *Makes 8 pitas*

1 (2¼-teaspoons) packet active dry yeast

1¼ cups warm water (110°F)

2 teaspoons salt

3 cups all-purpose flour, plus more for rolling

1. In a medium bowl, dissolve the yeast in the warm water. Allow mixture to sit for 10 minutes.

2. Stir in the salt and beat in the flour to form a soft dough.

3. Turn the dough onto a floured surface and knead until smooth and elastic, about 6 to 8 minutes. Do not let the dough rise at this point. Divide into 6 pieces; knead each piece for 1 minute and roll into a 5-inch circle about ¼ inch thick. Arrange the kneaded dough pieces on a greased baking sheet. Cover and let rise in a warm place until doubled, about 45 minutes.

4. Preheat the oven to 500°F. Bake for 4 minutes until the bread puffs up. Turn over and bake for 2 minutes more.

5. Remove each pita with a spatula from the baking sheet and add additional pitas for baking. Use the spatula to gently push down puff. Immediately place in storage bags.

12 DESSERTS AND BAKED GOODS

Many of my childhood memories of family get-togethers include a long table brimming with desserts. My wonderful family still loves sweets, and I've raided their recipe boxes to bring you some favorites that can be made from ingredients in your storage pantry.

Basic Pie Crust

For sweet pies, add 2 tablespoons granulated sugar to the dough. *Makes 1 pie crust*

- **1 stick butter, softened**
- **1½ cups all-purpose flour**
- **4 to 5 tablespoons cold water**
- **⅛ teaspoon salt**

1. Stir the ingredients together until well combined.

2. Shape the dough into a flattened disk; wrap in plastic wrap and refrigerate at least 30 minutes, or overnight.

3. Allow the dough to come to room temperature. On a floured surface, use a rolling pin to roll the dough to a 12-inch round. Ease the dough circle into a 9-inch glass pie pan, gently pressing it against the side. Trim the dough edge, leaving a 1-inch overhang. Fold the edge under and pinch to give decorative look.

4. Fill pie crust with filling and bake as directed. For a prebaked crust, preheat the oven to 425°F. Line the dough with foil and fill pan with pie weights (or dried beans, pennies, rice, or marbles). Bake the pie shell for 10 to 12 minutes, or until it is beginning to set. Remove the foil with the weights and bake 15 to 18 minutes longer, or until golden. If the shell puffs while baking, press it down with the back of a spoon. Set on a wire rack to cool.

Graham Cracker Pie Crust

Makes 1 pie crust

1½ cups crushed graham crackers (about 16 crackers; see page 147)

¼ cup white sugar

7 tablespoons butter, melted

1. Preheat the oven to 350°F. Mix the graham cracker crumbs and sugar together until combined. Add melted butter and mix with a fork until completely moistened.

2. Press into a 9-inch pie pan.

3. Bake for 8 to 10 minutes, until golden and the edges are crispy.

Chocolate Ramen Noodles

The noodles add a crunchy texture to this basic fudge recipe.

Makes about 40 squares

1 package ramen noodles (flavor packet discarded)

2 cups semisweet chocolate chips

2 tablespoons butter

1 teaspoon vanilla

1 (14-ounce) can sweetened condensed milk

powdered sugar, for dusting

1. In a medium bowl, break up the noodles into very small pieces.

2. In a small saucepan, melt the chocolate chips. Add the butter, vanilla, and condensed milk and stir well.

3. Add the crushed noodles to the chocolate mixture and stir until thoroughly mixed.

4. Line an 8 x 8-inch baking dish with foil and spray the foil with cooking spray. Pour the chocolate mixture into the dish and refrigerate for 2 hours, until hardened.

5. To serve, remove from the refrigerator and cut into bite-size pieces.

Chocolate PB Balls

Makes 36 balls (4 per serving)

1 cup chocolate protein powder

1 cup peanut butter

½ cup honey

½ cup rolled oats

extra protein powder, or powdered sugar or unsweetened cocoa powder, for rolling

1. In a medium bowl, stir the ingredients together to combine thoroughly.

2. Form the dough into walnut-size balls. Place on waxed paper.

3. Roll the balls in protein powder, powdered sugar, or cocoa (this will make them less sticky to handle). Refrigerate for 1 hour before serving.

Protein Granola Bars

Serves 9

1 cup quick-cooking rolled oats

½ cup vanilla or chocolate protein powder

½ cup wheat and barley nugget cereal (such as Grape-Nuts)

½ teaspoon ground cinnamon

⅓ cup unsweetened applesauce

½ cup honey

2 tablespoons peanut butter

2 eggs, well beaten

¼ cup unsalted shelled sunflower seeds

¼ cup dried fruit, chopped

¼ cup chopped pecans or other nuts

1. Preheat the oven to 325°F. Line a 9-inch square baking pan with foil and grease the foil for easy removal of the bars.

2. In a large bowl, stir together the oats, protein powder, cereal, and cinnamon.

3. In a medium bowl, combine the applesauce, honey, peanut butter, and eggs. Stir into the oat and cereal mixture.

4. Add the sunflower seeds, dried fruit, and nuts.

5. Spread evenly in the prepared pan. Bake for 30 minutes, until firm and lightly browned around the edges.

6. Let cool on a wire rack, then use the foil to lift out of the pan. Cut into bars or squares.

Country Berry Crumble Pie

Serves 6

1 Basic Pie Crust recipe (page 187)

4 cups fresh blackberries, blueberries, strawberries, or your choice

¾ cup granulated sugar

¼ cup all-purpose flour

½ teaspoon ground cinnamon

2 teaspoons lemon juice

grated zest of 1 lemon

1 teaspoon vanilla extract

CRUMB TOPPING

½ cup all-purpose flour

½ cup granulated sugar

½ cup (1 stick) butter, cut into slices

1 cup rolled oats

1. Prepare the pastry dough, wrap it in plastic wrap, and refrigerate for at least 30 minutes.

2. Preheat the oven to 375°F. Meanwhile, on a floured surface, roll half the dough into a 12-inch round. Fit the dough round into a lightly greased 9-inch deep dish pie pan. Trim the edge, leaving a 1-inch overhang; fold under and crimp.

3. Lay a sheet of foil over the crust and fill it with pie weights or dry beans. Bake for 15 minutes, then remove from the oven and lift off the foil liner and beans.

4. While the pie shell is baking, mix together the filling ingredients in a large bowl (berries through vanilla). In a separate bowl, work the topping ingredients into a crumbly mixture.

5. Pour the filling into the pie shell. Sprinkle the crumb mixture evenly over the top.

6. Return the pie to the oven and bake for about 1 hour, until the topping is golden brown. Don't let the crumb topping get too dark. If the pie begins to get too brown, cover loosely with foil. Remove from the oven and let cool a bit on a wire rack before serving.

Chocolate Éclair Cake

Serves 9

1 (14.4-ounce) package graham crackers

4 cups milk

2 (4-serving) packages instant vanilla pudding mix

1 (12-ounce) container frozen whipped topping, thawed, or 2 cups homemade Whipped Topping (page 210)

1 (16-ounce) container prepared chocolate frosting

1 teaspoon vanilla

1. Line the bottom of a 9 x 13-inch baking pan with one-third of the graham crackers.

2. In a large bowl, combine the milk and vanilla pudding mix, following the package directions.

3. Fold the whipped topping into the prepared pudding. Spread a layer with half of the pudding mixture over the graham crackers.

4. Add another layer of graham crackers, another pudding layer, and a final layer of graham crackers. Cover with a lid and refrigerate for 1 hour.

5. In a small saucepan over low heat, warm the frosting just enough that you can stir it easily with a spoon. Pour over the cake. Refrigerate for at least 12 hours, or overnight. Cut in squares to serve.

Auntie's Caramel Sauce

This delectable sauce can be used as an ice cream topping, to make caramel popcorn or caramel apples, or as a flavorful addition to pies and cakes. *Makes 4 cups*

1 cup (2 sticks) butter

2 cups packed dark brown sugar

1 (14-ounce) can sweetened condensed milk

2 teaspoons vanilla extract

⅛ teaspoon salt

1. In a 4-quart saucepan, combine the butter, brown sugar, and condensed milk; bring to a boil over medium-high heat until the mixture begins to thicken, about 2 minutes.

2. Continue to cook, stirring constantly, for an additional 2 minutes.

3. Remove from the heat and stir in the vanilla.

4. Serve warm. Refrigerate to thicken sauce.

Chocolate Sauce

Makes 4 to 6 servings

¼ cup water, plus 1 or 2 more tablespoons as needed

½ cup sugar

2 tablespoons cocoa powder

2 tablespoons butter

dash of salt

½ teaspoon vanilla extract

1. In a 4-quart saucepan over medium heat, bring the water and sugar to a boil. Continue to cook until the mixture becomes a syrup, about 5 minutes.

2. Reduce the heat to low, and add the chocolate, butter, and salt, and cook, stirring, until combined.

3. Remove from the heat, and stir in the vanilla. Allow to cool 5 to 10 minutes before serving.

Dessert Mousse

Serves 4 to 6

1½ cups milk

1 (6-serving) package instant pudding mix, any flavor

1 (8-ounce) container whipped topping, or 1 to 2 cups made from recipe (page 210)

1. In a large mixing bowl, beat together the milk and pudding mix.

2. Fold in the whipped topping until it is completely blended.

3. Spoon into individual dessert dishes and refrigerate to serve chilled.

Fried Fruit Pies

Makes 10 to 12 pies

2 Basic Pie Crust recipes (page 187)

2½ cups canned fruit slices or berries, or rehydrated dried fruit

¾ cup packed light brown sugar

1 teaspoon ground cinnamon

½ teaspoon ground nutmeg

¼ teaspoon ground allspice

1 tablespoon all-purpose flour

vegetable oil, for frying

ICING

1 cup powdered sugar

1 tablespoon milk or water

½ teaspoon vanilla extract

1. Double the basic recipe for a basic pie crust, wrap it in plastic wrap, and refrigerate for at least 30 minutes.

2. Drain the fruit and chop it into small pieces. In a medium bowl, stir together the fruit, brown sugar, cinnamon, nutmeg, allspice, and flour.

3. Allow the dough to come to room temperature. On a floured board, use a floured rolling pin to roll the dough pieces to a thickness of ⅛ inch. Cut into 5-inch circles.

4. Spoon ¼ cup of pie filling onto half of each dough circle.

Moisten the pastry edges with water, fold the dough over the filling, and press the edges with the tines of a fork to seal.

5. In a skillet, heat 2 inches of oil to 350°F. Fry the pies, a few at a time for 3½ to 4 minutes, or until golden brown. Drain on paper towels.

7. Stir together the icing ingredients in a small bowl. Lightly drizzle icing over the warm pies.

Sand Tarts

Makes 4 dozen

1 cup (2 sticks) unsalted butter

½ cup powdered sugar, plus more for rolling

1¼ teaspoons vanilla extract

2 cups sifted all-purpose flour

1½ cups chopped walnuts or pecans

dash of salt

1. Preheat the oven to 350°F.

2. Cream the butter. Beat in the ½ cup powdered sugar and the vanilla.

3. Add the flour, salt, and nuts, mixing well.

4. Form into small balls, as desired. Transfer to an ungreased baking sheet and place 1 inch apart. Bake for 30 minutes, or until golden.

5. Remove from the oven and roll on a plate of powdered sugar while still warm. Cool on wire racks and store in an airtight container.

Caramel Popcorn

Makes 16 servings

4 quarts popped corn

½ cup (1 stick) butter

1 cup packed light brown sugar

1 cup granulated sugar

¼ cup light corn syrup

½ teaspoon baking soda

½ teaspoon salt

1 teaspoon vanilla extract

1 cup peanuts (optional)

1. Preheat oven to 250°F. Place the cooked popcorn aside.

2. In a saucepan over medium heat, melt the butter. Stir in the brown sugar, granulated sugar, and corn syrup. Bring mixture to a boil, stirring constantly. Without stirring, boil mixture for 4 additional minutes.

3. Remove from heat, add baking soda, salt, vanilla, and nuts, if using.

4. On a shallow baking sheet, pour over popcorn and toss. Bake popcorn for 1 hour and 15 minutes. Allow to cool completely and store in an airtight container.

Easy Pumpkin Muffins

Makes 1 dozen muffins

1 package yellow cake mix

1 (15-ounce) can pumpkin purée

1½ teaspoons ground cinnamon

½ teaspoon ground nutmeg

¼ teaspoon ground cloves

1. Preheat the oven to 350°F. Grease a standard 12-cup muffin tin or line with paper liners.

2. In a large bowl, stir all the ingredients together until combined.

3. Spoon the batter into the prepared muffin compartments. Bake for 20 to 25 minutes or until a toothpick inserted in middle comes out clean. Cool on a wire rack.

Cinnamon and Sugar Tortilla Chips

Makes 32 chips

4 (7-inch) flour tortillas

3 tablespoons butter, melted

4 tablespoons granulated sugar

1 teaspoon cinnamon

Dash of salt

1. Preheat the oven to 350°F.

2. Brush the tortillas with butter on both sides and cut each tortilla into 8 triangles.

3. In a small bowl, combine the sugar, cinnamon, and salt. Sprinkle over the tortillas.

4. Place tortillas on an ungreased baking sheet. Bake for 2 minutes.

Apple Enchiladas

Makes 10 enchiladas

½ cup (1 stick) butter

1½ cups water

1 cup granulated sugar, plus more for sprinkling

1 (21-ounce) can apple pie filling

10 (7 to 8-inch) flour tortillas

cinnamon for sprinkling

1. Preheat the oven to 350°F. Coat the inside of a 9 x 13-inch baking dish with cooking spray or vegetable oil.

2. Combine the butter, water, and 1 cup sugar in a medium saucepan over medium heat; bring to a boil, then remove from the heat.

3. Working on a flat surface, spread 2 generous tablespoons of apple pie filling along the center of each tortilla. Roll up, enchilada-style.

4. Lay in rows in the prepared dish, seam side down. Sprinkle with cinnamon and sugar and then pour the sugar syrup over the top.

5. Cover with foil and bake for 35 minutes. Serve warm.

Crazy Cake (No-Egg Cake)

Serves 6 to 8

1 cup granulated sugar

¼ cup unsweetened cocoa powder

1 teaspoon baking soda

1½ cups all-purpose flour

1 tablespoon white vinegar

1½ teaspoons vanilla extract

7 tablespoons vegetable oil

1 cup water or coffee

pecans, chocolate chips, or toffee pieces, for topping (optional)

1. Preheat the oven to 350°F.

2. In a large bowl, sift together the sugar, cocoa, baking soda, and flour.

3. Make a well in the center and add the vinegar, vanilla, and oil. Pour in the water or coffee and stir until well combined.

4. Pour the batter into a lightly greased 8 x 8-inch pan. Add any additional toppings to the top of the batter, if desired. Bake for 40 minutes. Cool completely on a wire rack.

Peach Cobbler

Serves 6 to 8

½ cup (1 stick) butter or margarine, plus 1 tablespoon for the dish

1 cup baking mix (such as Bisquick, or made from recipe on page 209)

1 cup milk

2 cups granulated sugar, divided

1 teaspoon ground cinnamon

½ teaspoon ground nutmeg

1 (29-ounce) can sliced peaches sliced and drained

1. Preheat the oven to 350°F. Butter an 8 x 8-inch baking dish.

2. In a small pan, melt the butter or margarine on stovetop. Pour into a small bowl and set aside.

3. In a 4-quart saucepan over medium heat, mix the spices and remaining 1 cup sugar, with the peaches; bring to boil. Pour into prepared baking dish.

4. In a large bowl, mix together the baking mix, milk, and 1 cup sugar. Add the melted butter and mix until combined. Pour the batter into the pan over the spiced peaches.

5. Bake for 35 to 40 minutes or until golden. Let cool on a wire rack.

No-Bake Chocolate Cookies

Makes 3 dozen

3 tablespoons unsweetened cocoa powder

2 cups granulated sugar

½ cup milk

½ cup (1 stick) butter

3 cups quick-cooking rolled oats

½ cup crunchy peanut butter

1 tablespoon vanilla extract

1. Combine the cocoa, sugar, milk, and butter in a 4-quart saucepan over medium heat. Bring to a boil very slowly, then boil for no longer than 1½ to 2 minutes.

2. Using a big wooden spoon, stir together the oats, peanut butter, and vanilla in a bowl.

3. Pour the hot mixture over the oatmeal mixture and stir to combine. Form into small balls and drop onto waxed paper. Let cool until set.

Mandarin Orange Cake

Serves 9

1 package yellow cake mix

1 teaspoon ground cinnamon

3 eggs

1 cup vegetable oil

1 (11-ounce) can mandarin orange segments

1 (8-ounce) container frozen whipped topping, thawed

1 (20-ounce) can crushed pineapple with juice

1 (4-serving) package instant vanilla pudding mix

1. Preheat the oven to 350°F. Grease a 9 x 13-inch pan.

2. In a large bowl, combine the cake mix, cinnamon, eggs, oil, and mandarin oranges with their juices. Stir until smooth. Pour the batter into the prepared pan.

3. Bake 35 to 40 minutes, or until a toothpick inserted into the center of the cake comes out clean. Allow to cool.

4. To make the topping: In a large bowl, softly beat together whipped topping, pineapple with juice, and dry pudding mix until blended. Spread on cake.

Orange Jell-O Dessert Salad

Serves 6

1 (20-ounce) can crushed pineapple

1 (3-ounce) package orange Jell-O

8 ounces whipped topping, purchased or made from recipe on page 210

½ cup chopped walnuts or pecans

1. Drain the pineapple, retaining the juice for making the Jell-O.

2. Prepare the Jell-O according to the package directions, replacing part of the water with the drained pineapple juice.

3. Stir the Jell-O until it begins to dissolve, then mix in the drained pineapple and the whipped topping. Top with the chopped nuts. Chill overnight until the Jell-O is firm. Cut into squares to serve.

Homemade Vanilla Wafers

For chocolate wafers, replace the 1 cup granulated sugar with ½ cup granulated sugar and ½ cup light brown sugar; add ¾ cup unsweetened cocoa powder. *Makes 2 dozen*

- ½ cup (1 stick) unsalted butter, softened
- 1 cup granulated sugar
- 1 egg
- ¼ cup packed brown sugar
- 2 tablespoons milk
- 2 teaspoons vanilla extract
- 1½ cups all-purpose flour
- 1 teaspoon baking powder
- ¼ teaspoon salt

1. Preheat the oven to 350°F.
2. In a medium bowl, cream the butter with the sugar. Beat in the egg, milk, and vanilla.
3. In a large bowl, combine the flour, baking powder, and salt. Add to the wet mixture, mixing well.
4. Drop by spoonfuls onto greased baking sheets, spacing 2 inches apart. Bake for 12 to 15 minutes, or until the edges are golden brown. Move to a wire rack to cool.

Cracker Pudding

Serves 4 to 6

- 4 cups milk
- 2 eggs, separated
- 1 cup granulated sugar
- 1½ cups crumbled saltine crackers
- 1 cup grated sweetened coconut flakes
- 2 teaspoons vanilla extract

1. Preheat the oven to 350°F. In a 4-quart saucepan over medium heat, heat milk and stir frequently. Meanwhile, in a small bowl, beat together the egg yolks and sugar. Gradually pour egg mixture into the saucepan, stirring frequently. Allow mixture to come to a boil for 1 minute. Reduce heat to low.
2. Mix in the crackers and coconut. Cook, stirring frequently, until thickened, about 5 minutes. Remove from the heat and stir in the vanilla. Pour into a 1-quart casserole dish.
3. Using a hand mixer, beat the egg whites until soft peaks form. Spread over the hot pudding.
4. Bake for 10 to 15 minutes or until top is golden. Serve warm.

Cracker Pie

This was a favorite during the Great Depression. When baked, the filling takes on the flavor of soft apple pie. *Serves 6*

- 1 Basic Pie Crust recipe (page 187)
- 1¾ cups coarsely crumbled Ritz crackers
- 1¾ cups water
- 2¼ cups granulated sugar
- 2 teaspoons cream of tartar
- 2 tablespoons lemon juice
- grated zest of 1 lemon
- 2 tablespoons butter or margarine
- 1 teaspoon ground cinnamon

1. Prepare the pastry dough, wrap in plastic wrap, and refrigerate at least 30 minutes.

2. Divide the chilled dough in half. On a lightly floured surface, use a floured rolling pin to roll half the dough into a 12-inch round. Line a 9-inch pie pan with the dough, letting the edges hang over. Spread the cracker crumbs in the pie shell; set aside.

3. In a 4-quart saucepan over high heat, bring the water, sugar, and cream of tartar to a boil. Reduce the heat to low and let the syrup mixture simmer for 15 minutes. Remove from the heat and stir in the lemon juice and zest. Allow to cool for a few minutes.

4. Preheat the oven to 425°F.

5. Pour the syrup over the cracker crumbs in the pie shell. Dot with the butter or margarine and sprinkle with the cinnamon.

6. Roll out the rest of the dough into an 11-inch round; carefully transfer the dough round to the top of the pie. Trim the edges to ½ inch, fold under, press together, and flute. Cut slits in the top crust to allow steam to escape.

7. Bake for 30 to 35 minutes, until the crust is crisp and golden. Cool completely to serve.

Rice Pudding

Serves 4

- 1 tablespoon butter, softened
- 2 cups cooked white rice
- 3 cups milk
- 1 egg, well beaten
- ¼ cup packed dark brown sugar
- ¼ teaspoon ground cinnamon
- ½ teaspoon ground nutmeg
- 1 teaspoon vanilla extract
- dash of salt
- ⅓ cup raisins or dried fruit pieces (optional)

1. Preheat the oven to 350°F. Butter a 1.8-liter casserole dish.

2. In a large saucepan over medium-high, heat the rice

and milk and bring to a slight simmer.

3. In a medium bowl, combine the egg, brown sugar, cinnamon, nutmeg, vanilla, and salt. Mix and add to the milk and rice mixture. Stir well until all ingredients have combined, about 3 minutes. If desired, add raisins or dried fruit pieces into the mixture and stir. Pour the mixture into the prepared dish.

4. Bake for 15 minutes. Serve warm.

No-Bake Fruit Crisp

Serve this crisp in bowls with ice cream, as a breakfast topping for warm cereals, or as a sweet treat all by itself. *Serves 6 to 8*

1 pound peaches, berries, or other fruit

¼ cup (½ stick) butter

1 cup packed dark brown sugar

1 teaspoon ground cinnamon

¼ teaspoon ground nutmeg

¾ cup rolled oats

¼ cup sliced almonds

1. Peel and slice the peaches or other fruit as necessary.

2. Melt the butter in a large skillet over low heat. Whisk in the brown sugar, cinnamon, and nutmeg. Bring to a simmer over medium heat.

3. Stir in the fruit. Cook for 5 to 8 minutes, stirring frequently, until the fruit is tender.

4. Remove from the heat and stir in the oats and sliced almonds.

Sugar Cream Pie

Serves 6

3 tablespoons all-purpose flour

⅛ teaspoon salt

1 cup granulated sugar

1 cup heavy cream

½ cup evaporated milk

1 teaspoon vanilla extract

⅛ teaspoon ground nutmeg

1 baked Basic Pie Crust shell (page 187)

1. Preheat the oven to 425°F.

2. In a medium bowl, stir together the flour, salt, and sugar. Beat in the cream, evaporated milk, vanilla, and nutmeg to make a smooth paste. Pour into the baked pie shell.

3. Bake for 15 minutes, then reduce the oven temperature to 375°F and bake for another 30 minutes. Serve warm.

Chocolate Fudge

Makes 50 squares

2 cups granulated sugar

2 teaspoons light corn syrup

1 cup milk

5 tablespoons unsweetened cocoa powder

2 tablespoons butter

⅛ teaspoon salt

2 teaspoons vanilla extract

marshmallows, chopped nuts, or toffee pieces (optional)

1. Butter an 8 x 8-inch baking dish; set aside.

2. In a 4-quart saucepan over medium heat, combine the sugar, corn syrup, milk, and cocoa powder. Stir slowly until the mixture reaches the soft-ball stage, 8 to 10 minutes. To test for the soft-ball stage, take a spoonful of mixture and drop it in a dish of cold water. Grab the spoonful out of the water and squeeze between your fingers. If it is flexible and stays in a ball shape, it is ready. Add the butter, and salt.

3. Remove from the heat and allow the mixture to cool. When the surface dents when touched, slowly stir in the vanilla, marshmallows, nuts, or toffee, if desired.

4. Pour into the prepared pan. Refrigerate and allow the fudge to harden fully. Cut into squares. Store in an airtight container for up to 1 week.

Icebox Pie

Serves 6

1 (6-ounce) container frozen lemonade, thawed

1 (14-ounce) can sweetened condensed milk

6 ounces whipped topping, purchased or made from recipe on page 210

1 prepared Graham Cracker Pie Crust (page 188)

Mix together the lemonade, condensed milk, and whipped topping. Pour into the pie shell, smoothing the top. Chill in the refrigerator at least 1 hour before serving.

Basic Pudding Mix

Serves 4

3 cups nonfat dry milk

1¾ cups granulated sugar

1 cup cornstarch

¼ teaspoon salt

Stir all the ingredients together until well blended. Store in a covered container or in individual 1-cup packages.

To make pudding, place 1 cup pudding mix in a small saucepan. Slowly sir in 2 cups boiling water. Cook over medium heat for 3 to 5 minutes, stirring constantly, until the mixture is thickened. Let the mixture cool slightly and then pour into individual containers to make homemade pudding cups or into a single container. Cover and keep refrigerated.

Vanilla pudding—Stir in 1 teaspoon vanilla extract and 1 tablespoon butter once the pudding has thickened.

Chocolate pudding—Add 2 tablespoons of cocoa powder to 1 cup of dry mixture before cooking. Stir in ½ teaspoon vanilla and 1 tablespoon butter once the pudding has thickened.

Gingerbread

Serves 9

1 cup hot water

½ cup (1 stick) butter or margarine, softened

½ cup granulated sugar

1 egg

1 cup dark molasses

2½ cups sifted all-purpose flour

½ teaspoon salt

½ teaspoon ground cloves

1 teaspoon ground ginger

1½ teaspoons ground cinnamon

1½ teaspoons baking soda

1. Preheat the oven to 350°F. Grease and flour a 9 x 9-inch pan.

2. Bring the water to a boil in a small saucepan over high heat. Turn off the heat.

3. In a large bowl, cream the butter with the sugar. Beat in the egg and molasses.

4. Sift together the flour, salt, spices, and baking soda. Add to the wet mixture and mix well. Then add the hot water and beat until smooth.

5. Pour into the prepared pan and bake for 35 to 40 minutes, until a knife inserted into the cake comes out clean.

Italian Ice

For flavoring, add 1 cup of your favorite juice or 1 teaspoon of vanilla along with the water in the recipe. *Makes 2 cups*

2 cups water, divided

½ cup granulated sugar

1. In small a saucepan over medium heat, combine 1 cup of the water and the sugar, stirring often until the sugar has dissolved.

2. Remove from the heat, add the remaining 1 cup water and let cool for 20 minutes.

3. Pour into a freezer-safe container (I use a large cake pan) and place in the freezer. Add any flavoring and stir every hour for 5 hours, or until the ice becomes difficult to stir.

4. To serve, scoop into individual dessert bowls.

13 BEVERAGES

As previously mentioned, water should be the main liquid that you drink. That said, there often comes a time when you want something else. I do not advise storing a large assortment of sodas as they tend to dehydrate us more than hydrate. But having some stored for a special treat will be a nice morale booster. Drink mixes are also great for storage pantries. These days, there are many flavored mixes to choose from, including teas, fruit punches, and individual fruit drinks.

A great way to have fruit on hand for flavoring drinks is to dehydrate fruit slices such as lemons and oranges. Fruits can really lift a drink out of glum and up to "yum!"

Spiced Tea

⅔ cup instant black tea

1 cup powered orange-flavored drink mix

⅓ cup powdered lemonade

¼ cup sugar

¾ teaspoon ground cinnamon

½ teaspoon ground cloves

1. Mix all the ingredients together and stir thoroughly.

2. To serve, stir 1½ teaspoons drink mix into 1 cup hot water.

Mock Hot Toddy

1 tablespoon honey

1 teaspoon lemon juice

¼ teaspoon ground cinnamon

⅛ teaspoon ground cloves

7 ounces hot black tea

lemon wedge, for garnish

Combine the honey, lemon and spices in a mug. Add hot water and stir. Top with hot, brewed tea and stir again. Garnish with a lemon wedge.

Hot Cocoa Mix

2 cups dry milk powder

½ cup non-dairy creamer

¾ cup sugar

½ cup unsweetened cocoa

dash of spice such as cinnamon, nutmeg or cayenne or pepper

1. Mix all the ingredients together and store in a cool, dry space.
2. To serve, add 1 cup of warm milk or water to 1 to 2 tablespoons of cocoa mix.

Basic Almond Milk

1 cup raw almonds

4 cups filtered water

1. Soak the almonds in water for at least 4 hours. Discard the soaking water.
2. In a high-speed blender, blend nuts and the 4 cups water for about 2 minutes until the nuts are completely blended.
3. Line a colander with several layers of cheesecloth and strain the milk through twice. Leftover strained nuts can be use in baking recipes or to make almond butter. Almond milk will last 3 to 4 days. Adding a dash of salt can act as a preservative. Adding a dash of vanilla can make the mixture richer.

Oat Milk

8 tablespoons rolled oats

pinch of salt

1½ quarts filtered water

optional: sweetened coconut, agave nectar, or sugar, for sweetening

½ teaspoon vanilla

1. Place the oats, salt, water, and desired sweetener (optional), in a pitcher. Stir until mixed.

2. Allow mixture to soak in the refrigerator overnight.

3. After mixture has soaked overnight, pour the contents of the pitcher into the blender. Blend until well blended.

4. Pour the contents of the blender into a fine mesh sieve that is placed over a large bowl, and strain it thoroughly. Strain again if needed. The leftover strained oats can be cooked and used for oatmeal or used in baking recipes.

5. Add vanilla and stir.

6. Chill and shake before use. Oat milk lasts up to 5 days.

Rice Milk

1 cup uncooked white or brown rice

6 to 8 cups water

½ teaspoon sea salt

3 tablespoons maple syrup, agave nectar, or honey

½ teaspoon vanilla extract, plus more to taste

¾ teaspoon ground cinnamon, plus more to taste

1. Place the rice, 6 cups of water, and salt in a pan.

2. Cover and bring to a boil over high heat. Reduce the heat to low and simmer for 3 hours, or until the rice is very soft. (This can also be done in a slow cooker overnight on low heat.)

3. In a blender, puree rice mixture with the remaining ingredients. You will have to do it in 2 batches. Puree each batch at least 2 to 3 minutes to completely liquefy the rice. Add more water if you prefer a thinner consistency.

4. Strain mixture through a cheesecloth or a fine mesh sieve. Flavor with vanilla and sugar to taste. Chill, and serve over ice.

Old-Fashioned Root Beer

1 teaspoon active dry yeast

½ cup warm water

2¼ cups granulated sugar

1 gallon filtered water

3 to 4 teaspoons root beer extract

1. Dissolve the yeast in the warm water.

2. In a gallon size-jar, dissolve the sugar in the water.

3. Add the yeast mixture to the jar along with the root beer extract. Fill the jar with more

warm water and stir until all ingredients are well combined.

4. Cover jar and allow it to sit in the warm sun for 4 hours. The root beer will be ready to drink the next day. Chill before serving.

Vanilla Cream Soda

2 cups sugar

1 cup water

1½ tablespoons vanilla extract

1 bottle seltzer or club soda

ice cubes

1. Make a simple syrup by combining the sugar and water in a small saucepan over medium-low heat. Continuously stir and bring to a boil.

2. Once the mixture turns from cloudy to clear, take it off the heat and allow to cool for about 5 minutes.

3. Once mixture is cooled, add the vanilla extract and seltzer or club soda, and serve over ice.

Spiced Cider Mix

2 tablespoons sweetened lemonade drink mix

1 teaspoon ground cinnamon

½ teaspoon ground nutmeg

½ teaspoon ground cinnamon or 1 cinnamon stick

¼ teaspoon ground cloves

¼ teaspoon ground allspice

hot apple juice

1. Mix all dry ingredients together and store in a cool, dry space.

2. To serve, add 1 tablespoon of the mix into a cup of hot apple juice.

3. To make a large batch, add the entire mix to 1 gallon of hot apple juice in a large pan and bring to an active simmer for 5 to 10 minutes.

Amish Tea

3 cups boiling water

4 bags black tea

3 cups apple juice

⅓ cup honey

1. Pour the boiling water over the tea bags in a large heatproof container. Allow to steep for 5 minutes.

2. Remove and strain the tea bags and add the honey and apple juice. Mix well.

Citrus Tea

2 cups prepared orange-flavored
  drink

2 cups sugar

1 teaspoon ground cinnamon

1 (.15-ounce) package unsweetened
  lemon drink mix

In a pitcher, mix all the
ingredients together and stir
thoroughly. Chill for 1 hour
before serving.

14 ALTERNATIVE INGREDIENTS

One of the main reasons I am writing this book is to equip you with knowledge that can make you self-reliant during times when many won't be. Having the skills to prepare favorite recipes even when the grid is down will keep spirits up and tummies full. In this section you'll find do-it-yourself alternatives for common ingredients that you may not have on hand.

Bisquick Substitute

Makes 1 cup

- **1 cup all-purpose flour**
- **1½ teaspoons baking powder**
- **¼ teaspoon salt**
- **1 tablespoon vegetable shortening, added at time of use**

Stir together the flour, baking powder, and salt; store in an airtight container. To use the mixture, work in 1 tablespoon shortening.

Self-Rising Flour

1 cup all-purpose flour

½ teaspoon baking powder

½ teaspoon salt

Mix all the ingredients together and store in airtight container.

Powdered Sugar

1 cup granulated sugar

1 tablespoon cornstarch

In a blender, whirl the sugar with the cornstarch until it is powdered.

Brown Sugar

For dark brown sugar, add another tablespoon of molasses

1 cup sugar

1 tablespoon molasses

In a medium bowl, mix together the sugar and molasses until

completely blended. Store in an airtight container until ready for use.

Whipped Topping

Makes 3 cups

1 cup nonfat dry milk

1 cup cold water

4 teaspoons sugar

1 teaspoon vanilla extract

1. In a chilled medium bowl, combine the dry milk and water.

Beat with a chilled wire whisk for 5 to 10 minutes or until stiff.

2. Add the sugar and vanilla to the milk. Beat the mixture until blended, about 5 minutes.

Buttermilk Substitute

Makes 1 cup

1 cup milk

1 tablespoon distilled white vinegar or lemon juice

Mix together and allow to sit for 5 minutes. Use immediately in recipes calling for buttermilk.

Sweetened Condensed Milk

1 tablespoon butter

½ cup hot water

1 cup nonfat dry milk

¾ cup sugar

1. In a small saucepan over medium heat, melt the butter in the hot water and stir until combined.

2. Pour into a medium bowl and stir in the dry milk powder and sugar. Mix well until the sugar and milk powder are dissolved.

Homemade Butter

If you are off the grid, you can also pour the mixture into a canning jar and shake vigorously until the butter separates from the buttermilk.
Makes 1 cup

2 cups heavy cream

¼ teaspoon salt (optional)

1. Pour the cream and salt into the bowl of a food processor or blender. Process for 10 minutes, or until the butter separates from the buttermilk.

2. Press the butter into a small bowl with the back of a spoon to remove any remaining liquid. Save the buttermilk to use in cooking.

Butter Substitute

This has a different consistency than regular butter, but it can be substituted in cooking and baking. For a more spreadable butter, add another tablespoon of olive or sunflower oil to the mixture when processing.
Makes ¾ cup

¾ cup nonfat dry milk

⅓ cup water

¼ cup olive oil or sunflower oil

⅛ teaspoon salt

¼ teaspoon butter flavoring extract (optional)

1. In the bowl of a food processor, blend the milk with the water.

2. With the processor running, slowly add the oil through the feed tube until the mixture has thickened.

3. Add the salt and butter flavoring, if using, and process until all the ingredients are well incorporated. Refrigerate after use.

Easy Sour Cream

¾ cup raw unpasteurized milk, sour

⅓ cup butter

Beat together all the ingredients until mixture begins to thicken.

Heavy Cream Substitute

Makes 1¼ cups

1 cup milk

¼ cup nonfat dry milk

Whirl the milk and dry milk powder in a blender until thoroughly mixed. Use in baking or cooking dishes that call for heavy whipping cream.

Mason Jar Yogurt

Be sure to reserve 1 tablespoon of the yogurt as a starter for your next batch. To make a thick yogurt that has the consistency of sour cream, drain it in the refrigerator using a coffee filter. *Makes 4 cups*

4 cups milk (can be reconstituted from nonfat dry milk)

1 tablespoon plain yogurt (for your starter)

2 tablespoons nonfat dry milk (optional)

1. In a medium saucepan over medium heat, heat the milk until it reaches 190°F to 200°F. (Use a candy thermometer to monitor the temperature.) Take care not to let the milk come to a boil.

2. Quickly cool the milk to 120°F by placing the pan in a sink filled with cold water.

3. Whisk in the yogurt. To make a richer flavored yogurt, add a tablespoon of nonfat dry milk and stir well. Pour the milk and yogurt mixture into a 1-quart Mason jar.

4. To maintain the temperature and allow the cultures to activate, wrap the jar in a dishtowel and place it in a small cooler. Pour in hot tap water so the jar is submerged, but not floating. Close the cooler.

5. Your yogurt will be ready in 6 to 8 hours. If you prefer a tangier yogurt, allow it to sit in the cooler for an additional 2 hours. Store, covered, in the refrigerator.

CONVERSION CHART

MEASURE	EQUIVALENT	METRIC
1 teaspoon	—	5.0 milliliters
1 tablespoon	3 teaspoons	14.8 milliliters
1 cup	16 tablespoons	236.8 milliliters
1 pint	2 cups	473.6 milliliters
1 quart	4 cups	947.2 milliliters
1 liter	4 cups + 3½ table-spoons	1000 milliliters
1 ounce (dry)	2 tablespoons	28.35 grams
1 pound	16 ounces	453.49 grams
2.21 pounds	35.3 ounces	1 kilogram
325°F/350°F/375°F	—	165°C/177°C/190°C

SOURCES

Federal Emergency Management Agency, "Food and Water in an Emergency," August 2004, www.fema.gov/pdf/library/f&web.pdf.

Consumer Price Movements, December 2011, page 6, http://www.bls.gov/cpi/cpid1112.pdf.

Jeff Harrison, "Study: Nation Wastes Nearly Half Its Food," November 18, 2004, uanews.org/node/10448http://www.foodnavigator-usa.com/Business/US-wastes-half-its-food.

Federal Emergency Management Agency, "Storing Water in Plastic Soda Bottles," http://www.ready.gov/storing-water-plastic-soda-bottles.

American College of Sport's Medicine: Resources For The Personal Trainer, 3rd Edition, Wolters Kluwer, 2010.

United States Food and Drug Administration, "The Food Defect Action Level," November 2011, fda.gov/food/guidancecompliance regulatoryinformation/guidancedocuments/sanitation/ucm056174.htm.

Centers for Disease Control and Prevention, "Botulism," October 2010, cdc.gov/nczved/divisions/dfbmd/diseases/botulism.

University of Illinois Department of Food Science and Human Nutrition, "Nutrient Conservation in Canned, Frozen and Fresh Foods," October 1997, nutrican.fshn.uiuc.edu.

Federal Drug Administration, "FDA Recommended Pasteurization Time/Temperatures," 1998, http://extension.psu.edu/food-safety/courses/information/juice-haccp-resources/food-safety-juice-haccp-regulations/FDA%20Recommended%20Pasteurization%20Time.pdf/view.

US Department of Agriculture Research Services Division, Composition of Foods - Handbook No. 8, Analysis Charts Table 2 - Nutrients In The Edible Portion Of One Pound Of Food.

United States Department of Agriculture, "Jerky and Food Safety," November 15, 2011, fsis.usda.gov/factsheets/jerky_and_food_safety/index.asp.

United States Department of Agriculture, "Stable Food Safety," May 2011, http://www.fsis.usda.gov/PDF/Shelf_Stable_Food_Safety.pdf.

Rehydrating Dried Foods chart: http://nchfp.uga.edu/publications/uga/uga_dry_fruit.pdf.

Simon Kander, The Settlement Cook Book (Bedford, MA: Applewood Books, 1944).

INDEX

ACKNOWLEDGMENTS

To my husband—Through your encouragement, support, and love you have helped me see things within myself that I didn't know were there, and I am a better person because of you. You inspire me and mean the world to me.

To my children—You are and will always be my greatest achievements. Thank you for being my biggest fans and the best taste testers. I love you more than words can express. You guys are the best kids ever!

Special thanks to Kate Parker, whose suggestions made this a much better book than it might otherwise have been. Your work on this project has been invaluable and will be forever appreciated. Thank you so much.

ABOUT THE AUTHOR

Like many of you, I am a mother to young children, a wife, a sister, and a friend. But I find myself on a unique path of wanting to help others prepare for the unknown. Some say that a preparedness-based lifestyle is a life lived in fear, but there's nothing fearful about wanting to be self-sufficient or prepared for the unexpected. I have found that being prepared keeps fear of the unknown at bay. When unexpected situations present themselves, I'm capable of rolling with the punches because I'm confident that I have everything I need.

You may be asking how I landed on the preparedness path. I like to tell people that I tripped and stumbled right onto it. In 1999, I worked as a caseworker specialist for the Dallas chapter of the American Red Cross. I specialized in the Armed Forces Emergency Services Center and provided emergency communication between military personnel and their families. While working for the Red Cross, I was cross-trained in disaster management. On September 11, 2001 and in the weeks following, all of my training was called upon when my chapter became headquarters for coordinating with 9/11 emergency responders, victims, and their families.

This experience changed the definition of disaster for me. Disaster was only a theoretical contingency before 9/11, and then in an instant it became a reality. It was clear that the Red Cross was ready to manage a disaster, and an emergency call center was quickly established to deal with the aftermath. As I lived and worked through that experience, I learned how important it is to be ready for the unexpected.

Years later, I witnessed a different type of disaster—an economic one. Families are struggling each day to make financial ends meet. Many people have gone from having a satisfying economic lifestyle to being almost in poverty overnight.

I believe it is my purpose to help others become disaster-ready, building upon the knowledge I gained during my experience with the American Red Cross. This desire to help others find their preparedness path has propelled me further along on my own path, leading to the development of my website, Ready Nutrition (ReadyNutrition.com). Through the website, I've been able to introduce practical and easy-to-understand strategies for dealing with man-made or natural disasters and emergencies. And, as they say, "The rest is history."

The LORD is my rock, my fortress, and my savior; my God is my rock, in whom I find protection. He is my shield, the power that saves me, and my place of safety.—Psalm 18:2